FACE TO FACE

The Cross-Cultural Workbook

Virginia Vogel Zanger

NEWBURY HOUSE PUBLISHERS, Cambridge
A division of Harper & Row, Publishers, Inc.
New York, Philadelphia, San Francisco, Washington
London, Mexico City, São Paulo, Singapore, Sydney

1985

Library of Congress Cataloging in Publication Data

Zanger, Virginia Vogel.
   Face to face.

   1. English language--Text-books for foreign speakers.
I. Title.
PE1128.Z36   1985   428.2'4   85-5660
ISBN 0-88377-294-9

Cover design by Maureen Terrill
Photo search by Janice Miller

Photographs appear courtesy of Polly Smith: cover and pp. 2-3, 54, and 114; Donna Jernigan:
pp. xiii, xvi, 14, 68, and 86; H. Roberts Armstrong: p. xiv; John D. Stewart, FOCUS ON YOU: p. xv;
UPI/Boston Herald: pp. 28 and 146; Read D. Brugger/THE PICTURE CUBE: p. 42; Susan
Berkowitz, TAURUS PHOTOS, Inc.: p.53; Boston Herald American: p. 100; The Bettman
Archive, Inc.: p. 130; Wide World Photos: p. 131; Bill Brady: p. 146.

NEWBURY HOUSE PUBLISHERS
A division of Harper & Row, Publishers, Inc.

Language Science
Language Teaching
Language Learning

CAMBRIDGE, MASSACHUSETTS

Printed in the U.S.A.   First printing: September 1985
63-25955   7 8 9 10 11 12 13

Dedication

This book is dedicated to Dr. Carmen Judith Nine Curt, teacher, thinker, mentor, and friend, and to my new daughter Nina Marganit.

Acknowledgements

Several people contributed many useful ideas and suggestions for this book. Pixie Martin-Sharifzadeh, Consuelo Inchaustegui, Ned Seelye, and Ralph Radell deserve special thanks. My students over the years in the Boston Public Schools and at Boston University, and teachers throughout Massachusetts with whom I have worked on improving intercultural communication have also added immeasurably to *Face to Face*, and I wish to thank them. The idea for the book has evolved in the course of my work on several projects, and I would like to gratefully acknowledge the people who worked with me on them: Ellen Glanz, Libbie Shufro, Richard Berger, and José Masso, of the EdCo "Quienes Somos" program; Maria Perez, who worked with me on the "Project: Exchange/Proyecto Intercambio" curriculum; Miguel Satut, my partner in Cross-Cultural Strategies, a teacher-training team; Elizabeth Lantz of Newbury House Publishers, the editor who helped shape my first book, *Exploración Intercultural*, on which so much of the present book is based; and Professor Jaime Wurzel of Boston University, who generously gave of his time and support to discuss the intercultural concepts addressed here. I would also like to thank my editor, Jim Brown, and associate editor, Olivia Gould.

Finally, I wish to thank those members of my family who made this book possible: my South American families, the Sábatos and the Quiroz', my parents, and most especially, my husband.

To The Teacher

*"I like my ESL class. The teacher is good. But it doesn't really help
me communicate with Americans. That's what I'd like to learn."*

These comments, spoken in Spanish by a Central American student at a
Boston-area junior college, may reflect the sentiments of many other English
as a second language students. *Face to Face: The Cross-Cultural Workbook*
was written to bridge this gap between the classroom and the outside world.

For many students, confusion and ignorance about American attitudes,
values, customs, and nonverbal communication patterns account for the gap
between success in the classroom and actual communicative competence.
This book is based on the assumption that since culture is not inherited, but
rather learned, it can therefore also be taught. *Face to Face* gives intermediate-
and advanced-level English as a second language students a way to explore
American culture systematically. It uses an interactional approach to learning
about cultural similarities and differences: in structured interviews with
Americans, students find out for themselves about various aspects of
American culture. To ensure that students get the most out of their interviews,
the book provides questionnaires, background information, relevant vocabulary exercises, a framework for analysis and additional activities.

GOALS

1. Communicative competence

Face to Face helps students achieve communicative competence by giving
them experience conversing on a regular basis with native English speakers
in a controlled format and in a supportive atmosphere. Students are prepared
for each interview, both linguistically and culturally, through a series of
exercises and activities focusing on the topic of the interview. The interview
itself is structured carefully: students ask specific questions about both
customs and values that any American could answer. The questions
themselves are thought-provoking but non-threatening. Some are open-
ended, and students have to formulate one question (or more) on their own.

Face to Face is one solution to the ESL teacher's dilemma: how to get
students to practice their second language in a natural, " real life" context.
Using the book, an ESL class embarks on a common project: to collect data on
American life and to try to make sense out of it. Class discussions and
individual interiews thus serve a clear purpose beyond that of practicing

English. Oral skills improve because students use their second language to help them with issues that regularly confront them in adjusting to a new culture.

Students also have the opportunity to work on other basic skills as they research each topic. They practice reading narrative stories and short expository essays for comprehension at the beginning of every chapter. Writing skills are reinforced throughout the book as students think through and write out the answers to questions throughout each chapter. Further writing assignments are also suggested: essays, dialogues, research reports, and letters. Students must practice their note-taking skills as they record the most important information at each interview with an American. The interviews with Americans also provide students with a chance to sharpen their listening skills. Finally, such critical thinking skills as comparing and contrasting, making generalizations, and forming accurate conclusions are an integral part of almost every assignment.

2. Intercultural proficiency

Anthropologists estimate that language accounts for only 35 percent of communication. *Face to Face* introduces students to some of the cultural factors that can affect the other 65 percent: nonverbal communication, basic cultural assumptions, and values. Cultural factors such as these can mean the difference between (in the words of Leo Hickey) *knowing* a language and *knowing how to use one*, the difference between understanding *what is talked about* and *what is said*, and, ultimately, the difference between understanding and misunderstanding.

Intercultural proficiency involves more than an understanding of another culture. More important, perhaps, is an awareness of one's own cultural conditioning. Such awareness is not easily achieved because, in the words of anthropologist Ruth Benedict, "We do not see the lens through which we look." Therefore, some of the exercises in *Face to Face* are designed to help each student clarify just what his or her own culture stands for. Before interviewing an American on any given topic, the student answers all the same questions, according to his or her own cultural beliefs and customs, using an identical questionnaire. After the interview, the two sets of responses are compared and analyzed individually by each student.

Another way in which *Face to Face* helps students to become more culturally proficient is that it encourages them to see the diversity in American culture and in their own cultures. On any given topic, the opinions of a range of Americans — as many as the class can interview—are surveyed. A diversity of opinions and customs is bound to emerge, and students are asked to analyze these in several ways. First, they must summarize the most typical responses and discuss whether they represent the dominant American culture. Second, they must examine other responses and see where these fit in. Students are encouraged to be conscious of factors such as social class, age, region, ethnicity, religion, race, and gender, and how these can affect variation from the dominant American culture.

3. Attitudes and motivation

The social context in which students learn English has been found to be a very important factor in their success or failure. Research on second language acquisition suggests that how well and how fast students learn a second language varies with their attitudes toward the speakers of that language (Gardner and Lambert 1972). Whether or not students feel accepted or rejected by the speakers of the language that they are studying is also an important factor (Genesee et al. 1983). In fact, students' attitudes toward the target culture may be so important that a negative attitude can completely cancel out the effectiveness of language instruction, according to one researcher (Schumann 1978).

Face to Face seeks to change ESL students' attitudes by building their awareness and appreciation of alternate ways of seeing the world. The book's emphasis on values helps students to understand Americans' puzzling or possibly offensive behavior, for values explain *why* people do what they do. At the same time students are encouraged to examine and affirm their own cultural values. Only when people are sure of their own identity can they meet the challenge of adapting.

Many ESL students living in the midst of the United States are virtually isolated from Americans. If encounters with impatient clerks and strangers on the bus are students' main contacts with Americans, they may naturally wish to remain isolated. It is hoped that the outcome for students using *Face to Face* will be the motivation, self-confidence, and ability to break out of their isolation.

ORGANIZATION OF THE BOOK

Starting off is a short but crucial introduction to *Face to Face* for students. It is written to be discussed in class, if possible. It explains the rationale of the book in simple language, introduces the concept of culture, and asks students to identify their own questions about American culture. These questions should be compiled as a class list and discussed. They will help motivate the class, once students realize that the book is a useful tool to help them find the answers to their own questions. And at the end of the book, in the Choose Your Own Topic chapter, the class looks at their original questions again and discusses the answers in light of what they have learned. Therefore, the questions should be saved.

Starting off also cautions students against overgeneralizing and introduces the concept of ethnocentrism. It is quite useful if students understand these concepts well and can recognize them clearly, for they are bound to occur in subsequent activities.

Chapter Organization

The first 11 chapters are each focused on a topic, such as nonverbal communication, attitudes toward time, or youth culture. All the chapters have approximately the same format, consisting of three parts: Preparation, Interviews and Analysis, and Additional Activities.

1. **Preparation** for the interview includes the following activities.

- **QUESTION**, based on an opening photograph, is intended to stimulate interest in the chapter topic. The answer may take the form of a class discussion or an individual writing assignment.
- **PREREADING VOCABULARY EXERCISE,** a presentation of more difficult vocabulary used in the readings. Selected words are introduced in the context in which they are used in the readings, defined, and some exercises are provided.
- **CASE STUDY,** a short critical incident, followed by **QUESTIONS**. The case study dramatizes a cross-cultural misunderstanding related to the chapter topic. Questions check comprehension of the story and start students thinking about issues involved in the chapter topic.
- **BACKGROUND,** an essay, explains the case study and introduces some key issues related to the chapter topic.
- **PREINTERVIEW VOCABULARY EXERCISE,** similar in format to the Prereading Vocabulary Exercise, acquaints students with unfamiliar words used in the interviews.

2. **Interviews and Analysis**, the core of each chapter, includes in most chapters:

- **QUESTIONNAIRE 1,** a list of questions about the chapter topic, to be answered by the student, according to the customs and values most typical of his or her native culture. If there is time, it is recommended that students use this questionnaire to interview a classmate from another culture. This procedure offers several advantages. It builds understanding among students in the class, it provides practice for the interview with an American, and it gives them a chance to share, and thus become clearer on, their own cultures.
- **QUESTIONNAIRE 2,** a list of questions similar to those of Questionnaire 1, is a guide for students' interviews with an American. Space is provided for students to formulate their own questions related to the topic. Students are directed to write down any new vocabulary words that come up during the interview. At the end of the interview, students should fill out some information about the person they interviewed, such as age, birthplace, and ethnic, religious, or racial background. This information can later be used to help explain some of the answers.

Two of the chapters, MALE/FEMALE ROLES and EATING IN THE UNITED STATES, have a slightly different format. Three questionnaires are provided, each exploring a different aspect of the main topic. Each student interviews an American using whichever questionnaire interests him or her. In these chapters, students do not answer the questions themselves.

- **INDIVIDUAL ANALYSIS** is a list of questions asking students to compare and contrast their responses to their own Questionnaires 1 and 2, that is, the way they and an American answered the same questions.
- **GROUP ANALYSIS** is a list of questions to help guide the class discussion on the results of the interviews. This discussion is most important in making sure that students fully understand American responses. It also gives them the chance to find out what all their classmates found out in their interviews, which can help prevent students from forming stereotypes on the basis of one interview.

3. **Additional Activities** suggests further ways to approach the topic, such as:

- **ROLE PLAYS, ESSAYS, ETHNOGRAPHIC OBSERVATIONS, DEBATES, ADDITIONAL INTERVIEWS, RESEARCH PROJECTS, FIELD TRIPS, SPEAKERS, ETC.** These can be assigned according to student interest and time available.
- **IN CONCLUSION** is a question which asks students to reflect in a more personal way on some of the issues raised by their work on the topic.

Your Own Topic, the last chapter, provides students with the opportunity to research topics of their own, using the format of the other chapters. After formulating their own interview questions, interviewing Americans, and analyzing their data, students synthesize what they have learned by writing their own case studies. The case studies illustrate points of intercultural conflict that students identify through their research. Finally, students pull together all they have learned in the course of their investigations throughout the book by attempting to answer the original list of class questions formulated at the beginning of the book.

USE OF THE BOOK: SOME QUESTIONS AND ANSWERS

How much time should be allotted to using *Face to Face?*

Most of the activities are flexible enough so that the book can be used in any of three ways: as a main text, as a supplementary text, or as individualized work, according to how much class time is available. For a conversation course, the book can be used as the main text, with students doing most of the activities in class. If time is not a problem, students from different cultural backgrounds can interview each other in class using Questionnaire 1, working on the Individual Analysis together. For extra oral practice, students can role-play the Case Study. And of course the class can work on more of the Additional Activities with more time available.

If the class has a set of grammatical objectives to cover and time is therefore a problem, *Face to Face* can be used as a supplementary text, with the majority of the work completed for homework. It is recommended that

Starting Off, the student introduction, and Chapter 1 be done together as a class, to make sure that students understand the general procedure. After that, relatively little class time need be devoted to the book, except for the Group Analysis in each chapter.

If class time must be spent on other curriculum objectives, here are some suggestions for using *Face to Face* as a supplementary text. The entire first section of each chapter, Preparation, can be done individually, although the answers to the vocabulary exercises and the questions following the Case Study should be gone over in class. Similarly, students should fill out Questionnaire 1 on their own, interview an American outside of class, and answer the Individual Analysis questions on their own. The Group Analysis must be done together as a class, as must some of the Additional Activities, such as role plays. When much of the work is done outside of class, it takes on a journal-like character.

The book also may be used as the basis of an individualized student learning project, assigned to an individual student or to a small group of advanced students. Students' progress should be checked by the teacher. Individual students will not have as much of an opportunity to learn about the diversity of American culture as would an entire class using the book. So it is particularly important that the teacher monitor the conclusions drawn by individual students in order to watch for overgeneralizations.

What if students are timid about interviewing Americans?

For students' first interviews, the teacher may want to bring in some American volunteers to the class and divide students into small groups to interview them. This procedure may help break the ice, introduce students to the interview procedure, and even be used occasionally for other chapters as a change of pace.

It should be stressed that any American a student wishes to interview is acceptable, since we are all experts on our own culture. Students initially will probably feel more comfortable interviewing someone they know, but there is nothing wrong with going to the cafeteria or student lounge and asking a stranger if he or she would mind giving 10 or 15 minutes for an interview. Tell students that they will not be required to ask personal questions, so they need not worry about being embarrassed. They should explain to prospective interviewees that the interview is part of a class assignment to learn about American culture and to help them improve their English. If students choose to interview the same person for all chapters, that is fine, too, since they will have a chance to learn about diversity from their classmates' interviews. Finally, if some students are just so shy that they are unable to complete the interview assignment on their own, they should be permitted to join in a fellow student's interview.

What about stereotyping and overgeneralizing?

Stereotyping and generalizing are normal processes in all human cognition. They are dysfunctional and harmful only when rigid stereotypes and *over*generalizations prevent us from admitting any evidence that doesn't fit our preconceptions. And *negative* stereotyping prevents us from getting close enough to the object of the stereotype to perceive any contrary evidence.

The format of *Face to Face* discourages students from overgeneralizing about Americans on the basis of one interview, because they must examine the results of all their classmates' interviews before making generalizations. Although the number of additional interviews is not sufficient to make for a statistically significant sample size, the information gleaned from classmates' interviews can help students become more aware of American diversity. Obviously, it is up to the teacher to help students see when they are overgeneralizing and drawing inaccurate conclusions.

Face to Face seeks to minimize negative stereotypes through two strategies. First, it trains students to see the world from another cultural perspective, through another person's eyes. How? By encouraging students to constantly seek the explanations, the values, the rationales, the *whys* that underlie the differences they encounter. Second, in making students aware of their own cultural conditioning, they become more critical of their own value judgments. Students can learn to avoid imposing their values on another culture, the basis of most negative stereotyping, only when they are conscious of what their own cultural values are.

Finally, it is up to the teacher to point out, as many times as is necessary, that differences are just that, differences, but that no culture is better or worse than any other.

What is the teacher's role?

Clearly, *Face to Face* is not a conventional ESL textbook, and the teacher's role is somewhat different from that of source of all knowledge in the classroom. The teacher need not be an expert on cultural issues or even on American culture. Rather, the main responsibilities of the teacher who uses the book are to guide students in their investigations and to help them to draw accurate conclusions. Since students themselves have the responsibility for gathering their own data, teachers are not expected to know all the answers. If they want to supplement their own knowledge of cross-cultural communication, a list of suggested readings follows.

Can the book be used in EFL classes (outside the United States)?

That depends on whether or not any Americans are available to the students for interviews. If students themselves are not in a position to meet Americans, perhaps the teacher can arrange for volunteers to come to be interviewed by the class as a whole. Unfortunately, students would miss seeing the diversity of American life, but it would be up to the teacher to fill them in.

SUGGESTED READINGS

Condon, John, and Yousef Fathi. *An Introduction to Intercultural Communication*. Indianapolis, IN: Bobbs-Merrill, 1975.

Hall, Edward T. *The Hidden Dimension*. Garden City, NY: Doubleday, 1966.

Hall, Edward T. *The Silent Language*. Garden City, NY: Anchor Books, 1973.

Hall, Edward T. *Beyond Culture*. Garden City, NY: Doubleday, 1976.

Morris, Desmond, Peter Collett, Peter Marsh, and Marie O'Shaughnessy. *Gestures*. Briarcliff Manor, NY: Stein and Day, 1980.

Nine Curt, Carmen Judith. *Non-Verbal Communication*. Cambridge, MA: National Assessment and Dissemination Center for Bilingual Education, 1976.

Seelye, H. Ned. *Teaching Culture*. Lincolnwood, IL: National Textbook Company, 1984.

Stewart, Edward C. *American Cultural Patterns: A Cross-Cultural Perspective*. Chicago, IL: Intercultural Press, 1972.

Wurzel, Jaime. *Toward Multicultural Awareness*. Yarmouthport, ME: Intercultural Press, 1985.

PUBLICATIONS CITED

Gardner, Robert, and Wallace Lambert. *Attitudes and Motivation in Second Language Learning*. Rowley, MA: Newbury House Publishers, 1972.

Genesee, Fred, Pier Rogers, and Naomi Holobow. "The Social Psychology of Second Language Learning: Another Point of View," *Language Learning*, vol. 33, no. 2, 1983.

Hickey, Leo. "Ethnography for Language Learners," in *Foreign Language Annals,* no. 6, 1980.

Schumann, John. "The Pidginization Hypothesis," in Evelyn Hatch (ed.), *Second Language Acquisition*. Rowley, MA: Newbury House Publishers, 1978.

Starting Off

WHAT *FACE TO FACE* IS ALL ABOUT

An American is telling a joke. You feel good because you understand every word. All of a sudden, everyone is laughing. Everyone except you.

Has this ever happened to you? If you understood all the words, why didn't you get the joke? One answer is that words aren't everything there is to communication. The fact is that language is not even the most important part of communication: it explains only 35 percent. What, then, explains the rest? The eyes, the face, and the whole body all help communicate meaning. These are all parts of *nonverbal communication*. Also important is *how* the words are spoken. Finally, do the listener and the speaker see the world in the same way? All these things are different in every culture. So even if your English grammar is perfect, you will never understand what Americans mean until you know about their nonverbal communication and until you understand how they think.

Face to Face will help you to learn more about these parts of American culture so that you can communicate better with Americans. You will find out some of the ways that Americans are most like people from your own culture, and some of the ways that they are most different. The book will tell you some things about American culture, but most of it you will find out for yourself. How? By using the questionnaires in the book to ask Americans about their way of life. In addition to learning about American culture, you will also have the chance to practice your English and to get to know some American people better.

By the time you finish *Face to Face*, you still may not laugh at every American joke you hear. But you *will* understand better what Americans think is funny.

WHAT IS CULTURE? SOME DEFINITIONS

Question: Which of the photographs shows a meaning of *culture?*

The American flag

La Mousmé, by Vincent Van Gogh   A group of friends talking

The answer is all three pictures. Culture is more than just a system of government or art or a group of people. Culture is also the ways people communicate with each other. *Culture is the total way of life that a group of people share.*

For example, each culture decides:

- How people get married (their *customs*)
- What people teach their children about right or wrong (their *values*)
- What people think is beautiful (their *beliefs*)
- How people look at each other when they are talking (their *nonverbal communication*)
- What people study in school (their *institutions*)

What are some other things that every culture does differently?

Example: What people wear.

Some things to discuss about culture:

- Just as you cannot always see a piece of dirt on the sunglasses that you are wearing, your own culture is often invisible to you.
- Every human being belongs to at least one culture.
- Babies are born without culture: all culture is learned.
- All cultures are changing all the time.
- Most people feel that their own culture is best. This is called *ethnocentrism.*
- In fact, no culture is better or worse than any other culture. A cultural difference does not mean that one culture is right and the other is wrong.

- All people of all cultures have the same basic human needs, such as housing, food, love, and respect. Cultures have different ways of answering these needs.
- Cultural differences can make life both difficult and interesting.

When you study about different cultures...

A dog

Animals have four legs. TRUE OR FALSE?

This dog has four legs. But just because you know that one kind of animal does, you cannot *generalize* that all animals do. (Worms and snakes, for example, have no legs at all.) To say that all animals have four legs is an *overgeneralization*.

When you interview Americans and think about what they say, try not to overgeneralize. Find out what the Americans that the other students in your class interviewed had to say before you make any generalizations.

WHAT ARE YOUR QUESTIONS?

From the Americans you have met or seen, from television, books, and movies, you already know a lot about American culture. But you probably have some questions, too. For example, "*why* do Americans . . .?" Or: "Someone told me, but I want to know if it's really true that Americans . . . ."

On a separate sheet of paper, *without* your name, write down all the questions that you have about Americans and the American way of life, all the things you would really like to find out about how Americans think and act.

Your teacher will make a list of the questions from all the students. Discuss the questions in class. As you work through *Face to Face*, try to find some answers. Look at the questions again after you finish the book. It is hoped that the activities of this book will help to answer *your* questions.

Table of contents

Chapter 1

Gestures

Do you know what Americans mean when they use these gestures? Below each photograph, write what each one means to you. The photographs are explained in the Background section on page 5.

1. _____

2. _____

3. _____

4. _____

5. _____   6. _____

Preparation

PREREADING VOCABULARY EXERCISE

Study the sentences below. The words in *italics* are defined in parentheses.

> *borrow — index finger — gesture — misunderstanding — nod —*
> *obscene — palm — rude — shame — confused*

1. "May I *borrow* this book?" (to take something that will be returned at a later time)
2. She held her hand up, moving only her *index finger*. (the finger next to the thumb)
3. What *gestures* were made by the librarian and by Vu? (movements with the hands, face, arms, or body to express an emotion or an idea)
4. This gesture caused a serious international *misunderstanding*. (an incorrect understanding; a mistake in meaning)
5. Vu smiled at her and *nodded* his head politely. (moved his head up and down)
6. In Turkey, Greece, and Malta, it has an *obscene* meaning. (not to be used in polite company, usually because of sexual meaning)
7. In Cambodia and in Vietnam, the *palm* up gesture is used only to call an animal. (the inner part of the hand)

8. He did not understand why the librarian had suddenly become so *rude*. (not polite, not nice)

9. "You did something bad; *shame* on you." (a painful feeling that comes from knowing that one did something wrong)

10. The librarian looked *confused*. (not sure what is happening)

Directions

In each numbered sentence below, fill in the blank with the best word from the new vocabulary. Change tense and number (singular and plural) where necessary.

1. In the United States people point with the *index finger*, while in Puerto Rico many people point with the lips.

2. Pointing is a _____ that can be made with the head, eyes, elbow, lips, finger, hand, or foot, depending on the culture.

3. In many cultures, but not all, people _____ their heads up and down to mean "yes."

4. A quick nod of the head up that means "no" to some Greeks can easily cause a _____ with Americans.

5. In some cultures the gesture for "come here" is done with the _____ up and in some cultures it is done with the _____ down.

CASE STUDY

Vu Nguyen was a Vietnamese student studying English in the United States. He often visited his local public library to read the magazines and newspapers there. One day he found a book he wanted to read at home. So he asked the librarian, "Excuse me, may I borrow this book?"

The librarian answered, "Why, of course. Just give me your card."

Vu smiled at her and nodded his head politely. He wanted to show he was listening.

The librarian kept talking. "That book is wonderful. Isn't that author great?"

Vu had never read anything by the author. But he smiled and nodded again to show his interest. Finally, he said, "I would like to borrow this book today. Could you please tell me how to apply for a library card?"

The librarian looked confused. "Oh! I thought you said you already had one. I'll give you a temporary card for today. We'll send you your regular card in the mail. It will be about two weeks. Come right this way to fill out the application." The librarian held out her hand, palm up, moving only her index finger (see photo 1) to get Vu to follow her.

Now Vu was confused. He did not understand why the librarian had suddenly become so rude.

Vu smiled to cover up his confusion. As the librarian gave Vu the application, she said to him, "You look so happy. You must be glad about your new library card."

Questions

1. Do you think Vu was happy? Why did the librarian think so?
2. Underline all the words in the case study which describe gestures made by the librarian and by Vu.
3. Why did Vu nod his head?
4. What did the librarian think Vu meant when he nodded his head?
5. Why did Vu think the librarian was rude?

BACKGROUND

Some scientists believe that no single gesture has the same meaning everywhere in the world. Even a smile means different things in different cultures, as the case study shows. Vu smiled to cover up his confusion. That is one reason why a Southeast Asian smiles. But there are other meanings of a smile in Southeast Asian culture. It can also mean anger, happiness, politeness, or embarrassment. Vu's smile confused the librarian, because a smile usually means happiness to an American.

In a similar way, the librarian's gesture with her finger confused Vu. In Cambodia and in Vietnam, this gesture with the palm up (see photo 1) is used only to call an animal. To call a person with the same gesture is very bad, because it means that you think the person is like an animal. But in the United States, the gesture is not rude.

There was another problem that Vu and the librarian had. The librarian thought that Vu had a library card because he nodded his head when she told him to take it out. In Southeast Asian culture, you nod your head to show that you heard someone, to be polite. But in American culture, when you nod your head, it means you agree with the person, and it often means that you will do as they say.

In photo 1 on page 2 you can see the librarian's gesture that confused Vu. What do Americans mean by the gestures in the other five photos? Number 2 means "Great, perfect, acceptable, O.K." In other parts of the world, the same gesture has other meanings: in Belgium, France, and Tunisia, it means "zero"; in Turkey, Brazil, Greece, and Malta, it has an obscene meaning; and in Tunisia, it is used as a threat. Number 3 is used to show that someone is a champion or a winner, usually in sports. This gesture caused a serious international misunderstanding in 1959. Nikita Khrushchev, the Soviet leader, was visiting the United States and used this gesture, which means friendship in Russian. American newspapers printed it on page one. And the American people understood it to mean the opposite: that the Soviet Union would defeat the United States.

Number 4 is one of the few gestures which seems to be used only in the United States, and many people feel it is not as common as it once was. This gesture is made by moving one index finger against the other. It is usually used with children. Or adults do it as a joke. It means "You did something bad; shame on you." Number 5 is used in the United States, England, and Sweden to mean that the person is hoping for good luck. But in Greece and Turkey it means the breaking of a friendship, and in parts of Italy it means "O.K." Finally, number 6 means "defeat" or "no good" or "bad news" to Americans. Two thousand years ago, the people of Rome used the same gesture. Many gestures used today come from ancient times.

PREINTERVIEW VOCABULARY EXERCISE

Study the sentences below. The words in *italics* are defined in parentheses.

compare — insulting — item — laryngitis — stingy — waiter — native

1. *Compare* all the gestures. (look over two or more things and decide how they are alike and how they are different)
2. The gesture used by Americans to mean "come here" means something *insulting* to Southeast Asians. (rude, showing no respect)
3. Put a check mark next to each *item* below. (separate piece of information; a numbered question)
4. A friend has *laryngitis* and cannot speak. (an infection of the throat that makes it hard to talk)
5. Is there a gesture for *stingy*? (cheap, the kind of person who hates to spend money)
6. How do you call for the *waiter*? (someone who works in a restaurant taking the customers' food orders)
7. Do people in your *native* culture use gestures to communicate these ideas? (original, first, what you were born into)

Directions

In each numbered sentence below, fill in the blank with the best word from the vocabulary list above. Change tense and number (singular and plural) where necessary.

1. In restaurants in many parts of Europe, people clap their hands to get the attention of the *waiter* .

2. The same gesture is very _____ to an American waiter.

3. American waiters dislike _____ people who leave tips of less than 15 percent of the price of the meal.

4. If you cannot call, "Waiter!" because of _____ or some other problem, you must use a gesture to get his attention.

5. It is interesting to _____ the gestures used in different parts of the world.

Interviews and Analysis

• QUESTIONNAIRE 1 •
GESTURES IN YOUR NATIVE CULTURE

Part I

Do people in your native culture have gestures to communicate ideas 1 through 10 below? Put a check mark next to each item below for which your native culture has a gesture.

1. crazy
2. come here
3. hurry up
4. delicious
5. stingy

6. intelligent
7. be careful
8. be quiet
9. to call a waiter
10. to point at someone

Part II

What are some other gestures used in your native culture? Write down the meanings of five other gestures used in your native culture:

1. _____

2. _____

3. _____

4. _____

5. _____

• QUESTIONNAIRE 2 •
HOW AMERICANS UNDERSTAND GESTURES

Part I

Ask an American, **"What gestures do you use to mean crazy?"** If the gesture is exactly the same as the gesture for *crazy* in your culture, write *same* in the space next to item 1 below. If it is different, *circle* the item and learn to do the American gesture. Write down a few notes on the American gesture so that you can remember it.

Ask the American the same question about the other items listed below. Write *same* or circle the item, depending on what they say. If the American doesn't know a gesture for one of the items, write *none*.

1. crazy _____   6. intelligent _____
2. come here _____   7. be careful _____
3. hurry up _____   8. be quiet _____
4. delicious _____   9. to call a waiter _____
5. stingy _____   10. to point at someone _____

Part II

Look over the five gestures from your native culture that you listed in Part II of Questionnaire 1. Show each gesture from your culture to the

American you are interviewing. For each gesture, ask the American, **"What does this gesture mean to you?"** Write down the American's answers below.

1.

2.

3.

4.

5.

Part III

Now do the same for the gestures that you circled in Part I of this questionnaire. If your culture has a gesture different from the American one, show your culture's gesture to the American. Ask him or her, **"What does this gesture mean to you?"** Write down gestures the American didn't know.

Part IV

Ask the American to teach you some other gestures used in the United States. Try to learn them, and list their meanings below.

Person interviewed: _____

INDIVIDUAL ANALYSIS

1. When people make gestures, what parts of the body do they use? List all the body parts that are used in gestures. Next to each, write one gesture using that part of the body, and the culture it comes from.

   Example: the eyes — surprise (United States)

2. Are you always aware of the gestures you use? Explain.

3. Compare the answers on Questionnaires 1 and 2. What misunder-standings or confusions could happen between someone from your culture and an American because of gestures? Have any ever happened to you?

4. How can you learn what gestures to use in English?

GROUP ANALYSIS

1. In class, compare all the gestures used to communicate items 1 to 10 in Part I of Questionnaires 1 and 2. Include the gestures of all the cultures represented in the class as well as the gestures used by Americans. Below, write down any which you want to remember.

2. As the case study showed, the gesture used by Americans to mean "come here" means something rude or insulting to Southeast Asians. Are there any other gestures that are common in one culture but rude in another? List them below.

3. Compare the additional American gestures that you and your classmates learned from your interviews (Part IV of Questionnaire 2). List any new ones below.

Additional Activities

ROLE PLAY

1. Imagine meeting a friend who has laryngitis and cannot speak. The friend must use gestures to communicate during your conversation. In pairs, role-play this situation several different ways:

   a. with two Americans

   b. with two friends from another culture

   c. with an American and someone from another culture who don't understand each other's gestures

2. Role-play the case study at the beginning of this chapter. Role-play the situation two ways:

   a. as it happened in the case study

   b. so that Vu and the librarian come to understand each other

WRITING ASSIGNMENT

Based on the work that you did in this chapter, write your own case study about a cultural misunderstanding involving gestures.

RESEARCH

In a book called *Gestures*,[1] Desmond Morris and others at Oxford University in England wrote about the meanings of 20 gestures all over Europe. They also studied the meaning of the 20 gestures throughout history. Choose one of the 20 gestures, and look over the charts and maps in the book. Report on the gesture in oral or written form.

---

[1]*Gestures*, by Desmond Morris, Briarcliff Manor, NY: Stein and Day, 1979.

In Conclusion

As a result of your work in this chapter, have you noticed anything about how you use gestures when you speak? Will you have to change some of your gestures when speaking English? Explain.

Chapter 2

More Nonverbal Communication

Greek nephew and uncle greeting each other

Most Americans are not used to seeing men hug each other. Is it common in your culture?

Preparation

PREREADING VOCABULARY EXERCISE

Study the sentences below. The words in *italics* are defined in parentheses.

contact — deep culture — disappointed — greet —
nonverbal communication — proper — seem — uncomfortable — welcome

1. Some other examples are eye *contact*, ways of moving, and touching. (meeting; in this sentence: when two people's eyes meet; *physical contact* is when two people or things touch each other)
2. Gestures are a part of *deep culture*. (that part of culture which is part of a person, such as the way one walks)
3. Eva felt a little *disappointed*, but she didn't know exactly why. (sad, because something hoped for doesn't happen)
4. How did Mrs. Larsen *greet* Eva? (to say hello, with or without words)
5. Greetings and personal space, like gestures, are examples of *nonverbal communication*, or body language. (telling without words)
6. My brother would give her a *proper* greeting. (socially correct, polite)
7. But in person she *seemed* cold. (appeared, looked)
8. If someone stands too close, an American feels *uncomfortable*. (not comfortable, feeling that something is wrong)
9. She got a warm *welcome*. (a greeting to a guest)

Directions

In each sentence below, fill in the blank with the best word from the vocabulary list above. Change tense and number (singular and plural) where necessary.

1. In the United States, women usually ___*greet*___ their female friends by touching them on the arm, smiling, and saying hello.
2. Sometimes, there is no physical _____ at all.
3. Some American women kiss each other, but others feel_____ doing so.
4. To kiss a woman friend would _____ very strange to a Japanese woman.

5. The _____ Japanese greeting between women friends is a

bow.

CASE STUDY

Eva came to the United States from Peru to study at an American college. She wanted to live with an American family to find out more about the American way of life. And she wanted to improve her English.

The foreign student office of her college found the Larsen family for Eva to live with. Eva spoke with Mrs. Larsen on the telephone. She sounded very warm and friendly to Eva. She told Eva she could move in the next day. Eva was very happy about it.

Eva arrived the next day with all her luggage. She was excited to meet the Larsens. She rang the doorbell.

A tall, blond woman answered the door with a big smile on her face. She said, "Oh, you must be Eva! I'm so glad you're here! Let me help you with your bags. Come on in. I'm Hilda Larsen." She took one of Eva's bags into the house.

When they got inside, Mrs. Larsen put the bag down and stood across from Eva, about 3 feet away. She crossed her arms in front of her and asked Eva, "Tell me about your trip. I'd love to go to Peru someday."

Just then, her teenaged son walked in, hands in his pockets. "Jimmy, meet Eva. Maybe she can help you with your Spanish this semester," said his mother.

Jimmy said, "Hi, glad to meet you." His hands stayed in his pockets while he nodded his head.

Eva didn't know what to do with her hands. She felt uncomfortable. But she smiled and said, "Hi, nice to meet you."

The Larsens showed Eva her new room. Then they left her alone to unpack. Eva felt a little disappointed, but she didn't know exactly why. She thought Mrs. Larsen seemed so friendly on the phone. But now she wasn't sure. Jimmy also seemed a little cold, but maybe he was just shy.

Eva tried to decide what was wrong. She thought to herself: If an American girl came to stay with me in Peru, she would get a warmer welcome than that. My mother would give her a big kiss, instead of just standing there, on the other side of the room. And my brother would give her a proper greeting. Well, people told me that Americans are cold. I guess they're right.

Questions

1. How did Mrs. Larsen greet Eva?
2. How did Jimmy greet Eva?
3. Why did Eva feel that the Larsens were cold?
4. Do you think that Mrs. Larsen was cold? Why did she seem cold to Eva?

BACKGROUND

Many Americans shake hands when they meet someone. But to an American, the important things are the words and tone of voice. In other cultures, such as Eva's, a greeting is not a real greeting if there is no physical contact. A handshake or a kiss is a way of showing respect. And Asian greetings are different, too. In most Asian cultures, there is no physical contact at all in a greeting. Respect is shown by *not* touching the other person.

Eva used the "rules" of her own culture to understand Mrs. Larsen. But she misunderstood her. To Eva, Mrs. Larsen seemed cold because in Eva's culture a woman who greets another woman without giving her a kiss is cold. But Mrs. Larsen was not cold by the rules of American culture: she gave a warm smile and asked friendly questions. In fact, in Mrs. Larsen's culture, to kiss another woman when meeting for the first time would seem very strange.

Another reason why Mrs. Larsen seemed cold to Eva was that she stood so far from her. Scientists, mainly anthropologists and psychologists, have studied personal space, or how far from each other people stand. How much personal space people need to feel comfortable is a cultural matter. For example, Americans feel comfortable with their friends at a distance of 18 inches to 4 feet. If someone stands closer, it is too friendly and the American feels uncomfortable. If someone stands farther than 4 feet away, he seems cold. But Latin Americans and Arabs normally stand closer than 18 inches from their friends. In those cultures, standing farther than 18 inches seems unfriendly.

Greetings and personal space, like gestures, are examples of nonverbal communication, or body language. Some other examples are eye contact, ways of moving, and touching. Nonverbal communication is an extremely important part of conversation. Some scientists believe that people pay more attention to body language than to spoken language. For example, Eva thought Mrs. Larsen was cold even though her words were warm.

So, to understand what people from another culture really mean, and to communicate what *you* mean in another language, you must be aware of two things. First, you must pay attention to your own nonverbal actions. Second, learn the nonverbal ways of the other language. But both things are difficult to do, because of the way deep culture works. Most people are not aware of their own nonverbal communication because it is so much a part of them: it just feels like the only natural way to act. So to learn about another culture, you must watch carefully how the people act and how they react to you. In doing so, you may learn as much about your own culture as about theirs.

PREINTERVIEW VOCABULARY EXERCISE

affection — arm's length — backslap — to fit in — to greet — ethnic — normally — pat — observe

Directions

Study the sentences below. The words in *italics* are defined in parentheses.
  1. Mothers kiss their babies to show *affection.* (caring, love)

2. In your culture, when talking with a friend of the same sex, do you stand about an *arm's length* apart? (about 30 inches)

3. Sometimes American males give each other a *backslap* while shaking hands. (a strong touch on the back)

4. An American who is planning to study in your country for a year has asked you for advice on how *to fit in*. (to be accepted by others)

5. When two male college students *greet* each other in the morning, do they shake hands? (to say hello nonverbally or verbally)

6. How far apart from your friends do you *normally* stand? (usually)

7. Would a friend *pat* you on the head to show affection? (to touch or tap lightly)

8. *Observe* two Americans talking to each other. (watch carefully)

9. Do some *ethnic* groups act a little differently? (not from the dominant American culture, such as Italian-American, Afro-American, or Irish-American.)

Directions

In each numbered sentence below, fill in the blank with the best word from the vocabulary list above. Change tense and number (singular and plural) where necessary.

1. In Arab and Latin American cultures, most men stand closer than an

   _____ apart during conversation.

2. It is necessary to learn about American customs if you want _____

   with American people.

3. In the United States, friends _____ stand about 30 inches apart, but

   lovers stand much closer.

4. Most American men _____ each other by shaking hands.

5. Often, men also _____ each other on the upper arm as part of their

   greeting.

Interviews and Analysis

• QUESTIONNAIRE 1 •
NONVERBAL COMMUNICATION

Directions

Answer the following questions yourself, using the typical customs of your culture. Or, use the questionnaire to interview a classmate from another culture.

1. a. When two young men who work or study together greet each other every morning, do they always shake hands?

   b. Describe a typical greeting.

2. a. In your culture, when two girlfriends greet each other at a party, do they touch?

   b. Describe a typical greeting.

3. a. In your culture, is it O.K. for a husband and wife to kiss each other in public?

   b. If not, explain.

4. a. In your culture, when two female friends are talking, do they touch each other a lot?

   b. If yes, explain how.

5. a. In your culture, is it O.K. for a male to touch a female friend during a conversation?

   b. If yes, explain how.

6. a. In your culture, would a friend ever pat you on the head to show he liked you?

   b. If not, explain.

7. a. In your culture, if a mother gets angry with her small child, does she expect him to look her in the eye?

   b. Explain.

8. a. If a student looks his teacher in the eye while the teacher is talking, what does the teacher think?

   b. What does the teacher think if the student looks down while the teacher is talking?

9. a. In your culture, when talking with a friend of the same sex, do you stand about an arm's length from each other?

   b. If not, about how far from your friend do you normally stand?

   c. How do you feel when a person stands closer than the normal distance?

   d. How do you feel when someone stands farther away?

10.   Do you think most people in your culture agree with your answers to all these questions, or do some groups in your culture act a little differently? For example, do people from different regions, different social classes, different age groups, or different ethnic groups in your country have different customs? Give some examples.

Name: _____   Culture: _____

•QUESTIONNAIRE 2 •
NONVERBAL COMMUNICATION IN THE UNITED STATES

Directions

Interview an American with the following questions. Ask one question of your own about nonverbal communication. At the bottom, write down any new vocabulary you learned or heard in the interview.

1. a. In the United States, when two young men who work or study together greet each other every morning, do they always shake hands?
   b. Could you describe a typical greeting?

2. a. In the United States, when two girlfriends greet each other at a party, do they normally touch?
   b. Please describe a typical greeting.

3.   In the United States, is it O.K. for a husband and wife to kiss each other in public?

4. a. Do American women normally touch during conversation?
   b. If yes, explain.

5. a. Among Americans, is it O.K. for a male to touch a female friend during a conversation?
   b. If yes, explain how.

6.   Would a friend ever pat you on the head to show affection?

7. a. If an American mother gets angry with her small child, does she expect him to look her in the eye?
   b. Explain.

8. a. If a student looks his teacher in the eye while the teacher is talking, what does the teacher think?
   b. What does the teacher think if the student looks down while the teacher is talking?

9. a. When you are talking with a friend of the same sex, do you normally stand about an arm's length from each other?
   b. If not, about how far from your friend do you normally stand?
   c. How do you feel if a person stands closer than the normal distance?
   d. How do you feel if a person stands farther away?

10. Would most Americans agree with your answers to all these questions, or do some ethnic groups have somewhat different customs? For example, do people from different regions, different social classes, different age groups, or different ethnic groups have different customs? Give some examples.

11. (Your own question)

Person interviewed: _____ Ethnic background: _____

New vocabulary

INDIVIDUAL ANALYSIS

Part I

1. Can you see if someone does not like you from his or her nonverbal behavior? Explain.

2. Can you see if a person is crazy from his or her nonverbal behavior? Explain.

Part II

Compare the American's answers to questions 1 to 9 with your own answers to the same questions.

1. Write down the numbers of the questions which the American answered differently from you.

2. Write down the numbers of the questions which you and the American answered in the same way.

GROUP ANALYSIS

1. In class, compare all the Americans' answers to questions 1 through 9 on Questionnaire 2. Did all the Americans interviewed answer all the questions the same way? Which questions did Americans answer with the most different answers?

2. Discuss the questions that you made up yourselves and the answers given by the Americans interviewed (question 11). Which were the most surprising?

3. Compare answers on question 10. What ethnic groups in American culture have different customs, according to the Americans you interviewed? How are they different?

4. What are some cultural misunderstandings that could occur or have occurred between Americans and your classmates, because of nonverbal communication?

Additional Activities

ROLE PLAY

Role-play the situation between Eva and the Larsens. Then role-play the way Eva's family would greet an American guest. Finally, role-play the greetings in different cultures represented in the class.

OBSERVATIONS

Study American nonverbal communication more scientifically by doing one of the following observational experiments. Observe Americans in public places such as a park, cafeteria, student lounge, or in line at the movies.

1. Touching Observe two people talking for 10 minutes. Count the number of times that they touch each other. Use the form below. If possible, compare results with classmates who observed different people. Then figure out the average number of times of physical contact between Americans in 10 minutes of conversation. Discuss whether the ages, sexes, locations, or relationships between the Americans observed could explain their behavior. If you have time, observe people from other cultures to compare with the Americans you observe.

Location of observation: _____

Sex of subjects: _____ Approximate ages: _____

Number of times touching observed: _____

---

2. Greetings Observe Americans greeting each other. What are all the nonverbal behaviors in American greetings? Watch two males, two females, a male and a female, and a student and a teacher greet each other. On the chart below, put a check mark under the nonverbal behaviors that you see. If possible, compare your results with those of your classmates and present your observations together.

	smile	wave	handshake	nod	kiss	arm	pat	backslap
MALE-MALE ages: _____ location: _____								
FEMALE-FEMALE ages: _____ location: _____								
MALE-FEMALE ages: _____ location: _____								
STUDENT-TEACHER ages: _____ sexes: _____ location: _____								

WRITING ASSIGNMENT

Imagine that an American who is planning to study in your country for a year asks you for advice on how to fit in. Write a letter explaining about the nonverbal customs that he or she should know about.

In Conclusion

Which American nonverbal behaviors have been the most difficult for you to get used to? Explain.

Chapter 3

The Lessons of Proverbs

Students at Harvard University protest Harvard's financial investments in South Africa because of that country's racial policies, called *apartheid*.

Which one or ones of the following proverbs would you choose to go with the photograph?

1. The one that does not cry does not get fed. (Spanish)
2. Don't sell the bearskin before you sell the bear. (Italian)
3. The squeaky wheel gets the oil. (English)

Preparation

PREREADING VOCABULARY EXERCISE 1

Study the sentences below. The words in *italics* are defined in parentheses.

broth — efficiency — fairness — gander — hatch —
haste — origin — proverb — value

1. "Too many cooks spoil the *broth*." (clear soup)
2. In the modern factory system, *efficiency* is important. (getting things done fast)
3. Parents should treat all their children with *fairness*. (equal justice)

28

4. "Sauce for the goose is sauce for the *gander*." (the male goose, a large bird like a duck)

5. "Don't count your chickens before they *hatch*." (break out of the egg)

6. "*Haste* makes waste." (doing things too fast; rushing)

7. Many sayings in English have a Greek *origin*. (where something comes from).

8. *Proverbs* are like little lessons passed down from older people. (short popular sayings, usually of unknown or ancient origin)

9. An important American *value* is honesty. (something people consider important; an ideal)

Directions

In each numbered sentence, fill in the blank with the best word from the above vocabulary list. Change tense and number (singular and plural) where necessary.

1. The frozen foods in American supermarkets sell well because American cooks like *efficiency* in cooking time.

2. The most simple kind of soup is _____ .

3. Patience is not the important American _____ that it once was.

4. The majority of proverbs used in the United States are of English _____ .

5. Children have many fights because each child has his own idea of _____ .

10 COMMON PROVERBS IN ENGLISH

The following are 10 common proverbs in English. Each proverb teaches a little lesson: one value that people should remember. Next to the proverbs below is the origin of each one.

	Proverb	Value	Origin
1.	Blood is thicker than water.	**family loyalty**	Scotland
2.	Don't count your chickens before they hatch.	**patience**	Greece (Aesop's Fables)

3.	Sauce for the goose is sauce for the gander.	**fairness**	England
4.	Too many cooks spoil the broth.	**the individual**	England
5.	The early bird catches the worm.	**action**	England
6.	God helps those who help them-selves.	**self-help**	Greece (Aeschylus)
7.	Haste makes waste.	**patience**	England
8.	Time is money.	**efficiency**	U.S.A. (Ben Franklin)
9.	An eye for an eye, a tooth for a tooth.	**revenge**	Bible
10.	Never put off 'til tomorrow what you can do today.	**efficiency**	U.S.A.

PREREADING VOCABULARY EXERCISE 2

Study the sentences below. The words in *italics* are defined in parentheses.

caution — folk — ford — leap — original — wisdom

1. Many older cultures believe the value of *caution* is very important. (being careful, cautious)
2. *Folk* songs and *folk* tales often express the older values of a culture just as proverbs do. (popular; literally, "of the people"; traditional, old)
3. "If you don't know the *ford*, don't cross the stream." (a place where a river or stream is small enough to be crossed)
4. "Look before you *leap*." (jump)
5. They think it is more important to think of something new and *original*. (one's own, not a copy)
6. Proverbs are small bits of folk *wisdom*. (knowledge)

Directions

In each numbered sentence below, fill in the blank with the best word from the new vocabulary above. Change tense and singular and plural where necessary.

1. American teachers get very angry when their students copy from books

    because Americans believe it is important to write things that are

    _____ .

2. "Look before you leap" teaches the value of _____ .

3. "Oh, Susanna" is an old American _____ song.

4. A very old word for "stream" is _____ , but it is not used much in

   modern English.

5. In Oriental cultures the _____ of older people is more respected

   than in Western cultures.

BACKGROUND

Proverbs, sometimes called sayings, are examples of folk wisdom. They are little lessons which older people of a culture pass down to the younger people to teach them about life.

Many proverbs remind people of the values that are important in the culture, such as the 10 proverbs on pages 29–30. Values teach people how to act, what is right, and what is wrong. Because the values of each culture are different, understanding the values of another culture helps explain how people think and act. Understanding your own cultural values is important too. If you can accept that people from other cultures act according to *their* values, not *yours*, getting along with them will be much easier.

Many proverbs are very old. So some of the values they teach may not be as important in the culture as they once were. For example, Americans today do not pay much attention to the proverb "Haste makes waste" because patience is not important to them. But if you know about past values, it helps you to understand the present. And many of the older values are still strong today. Benjamin Franklin, a famous American diplomat, writer, and scientist, died in 1790. But his proverb "Time is money" is taken more seriously by Americans of today than ever before.

A study of proverbs from around the world shows that some values are shared by many cultures. In many cases, though, the same idea is expressed differently. Two examples are the proverbs mentioned at the beginning of this chapter: "The squeaky wheel gets the oil" and "He who does not cry does not get fed." Both teach this lesson: it is important to make people know what you want, which is the value of *assertiveness*. Another example is the value of *caution*, which many older cultures believe is very important. The importance of being cautious is communicated in seven different ways by the following proverbs: "Turn the tongue seven times, then speak" (French); "Have an umbrella before getting wet" (Japanese); "Before you drink the soup, blow on it" (Arabic); "First weigh [the consequences], then dare" (German); "If you don't know the ford, don't cross the stream" (Russian); "Be careful bending your head—you may break it" (Italian); "Look before you leap" (English).

While English proverbs are part of the oral culture in the United States, they are not often used in writing. In other cultures, proverbs can be very useful and important in writing. Good writers in Chinese often begin an essay with a Chinese proverb. It shows knowledge of the past, an important Chinese value. But Americans do not value the past as much as the Chinese do. They think it is more important to think of something new and original. So a good writer in English will try to explain ideas in a new way and not use English proverbs if possible. But translating proverbs from other languages is accepted in English writing.

Interviews and Analysis

•QUESTIONNAIRE 1 •
PROVERBS

Directions

Answer the following questions about proverbs in your native language. If possible, interview an older person from your native culture. Give a few examples of proverbs first. Or, interview a classmate who speaks a different language, using the following guidelines.

1. a. Write a proverb in your native language:

b. Translate it word by word:

c. Give an example of a situation where you would use it:

d. Explain what it really means:

e. Does the proverb teach a value? Write it:

f. Is the proverb used often today?

g. Do you know its origin, where it comes from?

2. a. Write a second proverb in your native language:

b. Translation:

c. Situation:

d. Meaning:

e. Value:

f. Is it used today?

g. Origin:

3. a. Write a third proverb in your native language:

b. Translation:

c. Situation:

d. Meaning:

e. Value:

f. Is it used today?

g. Origin:

4. a. Write a fourth proverb in your native language:

b. Translation:

c. Situation:

d. Meaning:

e. Value:

f. Is it used today?

g. Origin:

Name:_____ Language: _____ Place of birth: _____

• QUESTIONNAIRE 2 •
PROVERBS IN ENGLISH

Directions

Interview an American to find out about four American proverbs. Use the following questionnaire. Do not use any of the 10 English proverbs listed on pages 29–30. Since older people often know more proverbs, try to interview someone older. At the end of the interview form below, write down any new vocabulary that you learned during the interview.

1. a. Tell me a proverb in English, such as "Haste makes waste."

   b. In what situation would you use it?

   c. What does it mean, or what is its message?

   d. Does it teach a value, such as patience or caution?

   e. If yes, do you think that value is still considered important by most Americans today?

   f. Is the proverb used much today?

g. Do you know the origin of the proverb (the Bible, for example)?

2. a. Tell me a second proverb in English.

b. In what situation would you use it?

c. What does it mean, or what is its message?

d. Does it teach a value, such as patience or caution?

e. If yes, do you think that value is still considered important by most Americans today?

f. Is the proverb used much today?

g. Do you know the origin of the proverb (the Bible, for example)?

3. a. Tell me another proverb in English.

b. In what situations would you use it?

c. What does it mean, or what is its message?

d. Does it teach a value, such as patience or caution?

e. If yes, do you think that value is still considered important by most Americans today?

f. Is the proverb used much today?

g. Do you know the origin of the proverb (the Bible, for example)?

4. a. Please tell me one more proverb in English.

b. In what situations would you use it?

c. What does it mean, or what is its message?

d. Does it teach a value?

e. If yes, do you think that value is still considered important by most Americans today?

f. Is the proverb used much today?

g. Do you know the origin of the proverb (the Bible, for example)?

Person interviewed: _____

New vocabulary

INDIVIDUAL ANALYSIS

1. Look over the four proverbs in English on Questionnaire 2. Are there any proverbs in your native language that mean something similar, or that people would use in the same kind of situation? Below, write the similar proverb or proverbs in your native language, then translate into English. Write the English proverb it is similar to.

2. Review the values of the proverbs in English that you wrote down on Questionnaire 2. Is there any one which seems to you to be typically American? Explain.

GROUP ANALYSIS

(Note: If possible, before the class discussion on proverbs, the teacher should collect both native language and English proverbs from students and compile two lists to distribute for the class discussion.)

1. In class, share one proverb translated from your native language which you feel reflects a value which is very important in your culture. Before explaining the meaning, see if your classmates can guess it correctly.

2. Discuss the similarities and differences among the cultures represented in the class, based on one proverb from each student.

3. List below some of the English language proverbs that you liked the best which were collected by your classmates.

4. Discuss in class any of the proverbs that you do not understand.

5. What American values are reflected by the English language proverbs collected by the class? List any value which occurred in more than one proverb:

Additional Activities

ROLE PLAY

In class, form small groups. Choose one proverb in English, and make up a skit about a situation which the proverb would fit. Perform the skit and see if your classmates can guess which American proverb applies to your skit.

WRITING ASSIGNMENT

Choose a proverb from your native language that has special meaning for you. Write an essay about the truth or meaning of the proverb. Give examples from your own experience that support the truth of the proverb.

ADDITIONAL RESEARCH

Folk songs, folk tales, fables, and traditional children's stories such as fairy tales often express the older values of a culture just as proverbs do. Select an old American folk song, children's tale, or fable. Try to find out where it came from and when. Then copy or summarize it. What is its lesson, or moral? If the hero or heroine has any special qualities that you think might be old American values, what are they? Do you think the values in the story or song are still important in American society today? Present your report in oral or written form.

ADDITIONAL PROVERBS

Collect 10 more American proverbs, analyzing them as you did on Questionnaire 2.

In Conclusion

Write down five values that are the most important in your culture today:

Write five values that used to be important in your culture:

Chapter 4

To Be Polite

A group of friends share a meal at a party.

If you were a guest at this party, what are two things that you would do to be polite? What are two things you definitely would *not* do?

Preparation

PREREADING VOCABULARY EXERCISE

Study the sentences below. The words in *italics* are defined in parentheses.

alcohol — guest — host — impolite — informal — invitation — slang

1. Some religious groups do not drink *alcohol.* (beer, wine, or other kinds of liquor)

2. John tried hard to be a polite *guest* according to the rules of his culture. (someone visiting another person's home)

3. When John got to the party, his *host* greeted him at the door in a very friendly way. (the person giving a party)

4. What is polite in one culture is sometimes quite *impolite* in another culture. (not polite; rude; not nice)

5. Most Americans think it is important to be *informal*. (not fancy or formal; casual; without ceremony)

6. Some American party *invitations* ask the guests to bring their own liquor. (a written or spoken way to ask someone to come to something)

7. "Booze" is a *slang* expression for liquor. (language not used in formal situations or in writing, and not often found in the dictionary)

DIRECTIONS

In each numbered sentence, fill in the blank with the best word from the vocabulary list above. Change tense and number (singular and plural) where necessary.

1. In the United States, some weddings have 500 _____ while other weddings are for family only.

2. At formal American weddings, guests wear very fancy clothes, but other weddings are more _____ .

3. If you are invited to an American wedding, it is _____ not to let the family know if you cannot come.

4. A _____ expression for "to get married" is "to tie the knot."

5. Many times if the party after a wedding is in a church, no _____ is served.

CASE STUDY

John, an American, was happy when his Saudi Arabian neighbor invited him to a party at his apartment, just down the hall in the same apartment building. John left work early the night of the party to buy something to bring. He made a special trip to the neighborhood liquor store to buy a bottle of his favorite white wine for the party.

When John got to the party, his host, Mazen, greeted him at the door in a friendly way. He put his arm around John's shoulders and said, "Oh, John. I'm so glad you could come."

John answered, "How're you doing, Mazen? Looks like a great party. Here, I brought you some of my favorite wine."

Mazen took the wine but said nothing about it. Then he said, "I'd like you to meet my sister who came from Riad, my city, just two days ago."

John reached out to shake Mazen's sister's hand, but she just stood there, and stopped smiling. John decided that she was probably shy. So he tried to be especially friendly to her. They had a nice conversation until Mazen ended it.

John was saying to Mazen's sister, "So, it looks like your brother is going to show you the town." Because John was feeling very friendly to his host and his host's sister, he put one arm around each of them. Mazen suddenly looked very serious.

He stood up and took John by the arm and said, "Come over here and try some of our food."

John enjoyed himself very much at the party that night. He couldn't believe how much food Mazen had prepared. As he was leaving, he realized that he had not seen his bottle of wine. He decided that in all the confusion, Mazen had probably forgotten to open it.

Questions

1. Why did John buy the wine?
2. Why didn't Mazen open it?
3. Why didn't Mazen say anything to John about the wine?
4. Why didn't Mazen's sister shake hands with John?
5. Why did John put his arm around Mazen and his sister?
6. Why did Mazen suddenly end John's conversation with his sister?

BACKGROUND

What is polite in one culture is sometimes impolite in another culture. In the case study, John tried hard to be a polite guest according to the rules of his culture. In the United States, people often bring wine or beer to a party. In fact, the invitations to many American parties have the letters "B.Y.O.B.," which means "Bring your own booze" ("booze" is a slang expression for alcohol). However, most Moslems, like Mazen, do not drink alcohol. Their religion forbids it. So John's wine was not welcome at the party, although his host was too polite to say so. (Even in the United States it is not always a good idea to bring alcohol: most states do not allow anyone under the age of 18 or 21 to buy alcohol, and some religious groups forbid it.)

John also showed little understanding of Arab culture when he tried to shake hands with Mazen's sister. By American customs, he was just trying to be polite. But in Moslem cultures, the most impolite thing a man can do is to touch a woman who is not his wife. John put his arm around Mazen and his sister to show his friendship. But to an Arab, that gesture would show the opposite: that John did not respect his sister. For that reason it was an insult to Mazen as well.

People all over the world want respect from others. But cultures show respect in different ways, as John's experiences at Mazen's party show. Some of these differences are explained by the values that each culture thinks are important. For example, the American custom of "B.Y.O.B." can be explained by the fact that most Americans think it is important to be informal and direct. And Mazen did not serve wine at his party because one of the most important Saudi values is living by the laws of the Moslem religion.

PREINTERVIEW VOCABULARY EXERCISE

Study the sentences below. The words in *italics* are defined in parentheses.

generosity — hospitality — prayer — table manners — toast

1. An example of *generosity* is giving money to the poor. (giving freely of one's time or money; being generous)
2. Giving parties is one way that people show their *hospitality*. (making guests feel welcome; friendliness to guests)
3. Will there be a *prayer* before the meal? (silent or spoken communication to God; the act of praying)
4. Eating with the left hand is seen as bad *table manners* in Arab cultures. (eating customs)
5. Is there a *toast* before the meal? (with drinking glasses lifted, a few words said in honor of someone or something)

Directions

In each numbered sentence, fill in the blank with the best word from the above vocabulary list. Change tense and singular and plural where necessary.

1. "Salud," meaning "health," is a popular Spanish _*toast*_ .

2. "My house is your house" is a Spanish proverb showing the importance of _____ in that culture.

3. In cultures where _____ is an important value, one never eats in front of others without first offering them some food.

4. Some Americans say a _____ before a meal; this is sometimes known as "saying grace."

5. Talking with your mouth full is bad _____ in many, but not all, cultures.

Interviews and Analysis

• QUESTIONNAIRE 1 •
TO BE POLITE

Imagine that you are invited to a party given by a friend from your culture. Answer the following questions according to the customs of your culture. To answer each question, make a check mark under the "yes" or "no" column to the right of the question, and then note down any explanation in the space provided.

	YES	NO

1. Imagine that you are invited to a small graduation party given by a friend from your culture. Do you bring along something to eat or drink? Explain. _____

2. You bring your friend a gift for his graduation. Do you expect him to open it during the party? Explain. _____

3. At the party, your friend introduces you to his cousin, a woman who is about thirty years old. Is it polite to call her by her first name?

4. Your friend's cousin invites you to a party at her house next week, but you know that you will be busy then. Do you tell her you will come anyway, just to be polite? Explain. _____

5. You take out a pack of cigarettes. To be polite, do you offer them first to your friend and his cousin? Explain. _____

6. You are thirsty. Do you ask your host for a drink? Explain. _____

	YES	NO

7. You tell your friend how much you like his house. Do you ask him how much it cost or how much he pays in rent? Explain. _____
_____

8. Everyone sits down to eat together. Is there a prayer or a toast before the meal? Explain.
_____

9. The food is delicious, but you are not hungry. Do you finish everything on your plate, to be polite?

10. If you want a little more food, is it polite to ask for more?

11. If your host asks you if you want more to eat, do you first say "no" to be polite? Explain._____
_____

12. After dinner, do you help take the dishes to the kitchen, to be polite? Explain. _____
_____

13. After eating, everyone leaves the table to relax. Are you shocked when your host rests his feet in front of him on a low table or chair? Explain.
_____

14. Several days after the party, you want to tell your friend what a good time you had. Is it impolite to go over to his house, without calling first? Explain. _____
_____

Name: _____　Culture: _____

• QUESTIONNAIRE 2 •
TO BE POLITE IN THE UNITED STATES

Interview an American with the following questionnaire. Ask the person to try to answer the questions yes or no. Make up one question of your own. Write down any new vocabulary that you learned during the interview at the end of the questionnaire.

	YES	NO

1. Imagine that you are invited to a small gradu-ation party given by an American friend. Do you bring along something to eat or drink? Explain.

   _____

   _____

2. You bring your friend a gift for his graduation. Do you expect him to open it during the party? Explain. _____

   _____

3. At the party, your friend introduces you to his cousin, a woman who is about 30 years old. Is it polite to call her by her first name?

4. Your friend's cousin invites you to a party at her house next week, but you know that you will be busy then. Do you tell her you will come anyway, just to be polite? Explain. _____

   _____

5. You take out a pack of cigarettes. To be polite, do you offer them first to your friend and his cousin? Explain. _____

   _____

6. You are thirsty. Do you ask your host for a drink? Explain. _____

   _____

7. You tell your friend how much you like his house. Do you ask him how much it cost or how much he pays in rent? Explain. _____

   _____

	YES	NO

8. Everyone sits down to eat together. Is there a prayer or a toast before the meal? Explain.

_____

_____

9. The food is delicious, but you are not hungry. Do you finish everything on your plate, to be polite?

10. If you want a little more food, is it polite to ask for more?

11. If your host asks you if you want more to eat, do you first say "no" to be polite? Explain. _____

_____

12. After dinner, do you help take the dishes to the kitchen to be polite? Explain. _____

_____

13. After eating, everyone leaves the table to relax. Are you shocked when your host rests his feet in front of him on a low table or chair? Explain.

_____

_____

14. Several days after the party, you want to tell your friend what a good time you had. Is it impolite to go to his house, without calling first? Explain. _____

_____

15. (Your own question)

Person interviewed: _____

New vocabulary

INDIVIDUAL ANALYSIS

Compare the yes/no answers that you wrote down on Questionnaires 1 and 2.

1. How many of the same questions received the same yes or no response on both questionnaires?

2. In the space below, write the number of each question that received *different* responses, that is, "yes" on one questionnaire and "no" on another.

3. Choose one question from those that you listed above in question 2, and explain the answers if you can.

4. Choose one of the customs from Questionnaire 1 and explain it in terms of one value that is important in your culture (for example, generosity, hospitality, religion).

5. Choose one of the customs from Questionnaire 2 and explain it in terms of one value that is important in American culture.

GROUP ANALYSIS

In class, compare the different answers from Americans interviewed with Questionnaire 2.

1. Did all the Americans interviewed respond with the same yes/no answers to all the questions?

2. For those questions to which some Americans answered "yes" and some "no," compare the explanations they gave for their answers.

3. Discuss the questions that each student made up and the answers given by the Americans interviewed.

4. Review the responses that you and your classmates gave to question 5 of the Individual Analysis, the question about American values.

Additional Activities

ROLE PLAY

Practice using your understanding of polite behavior in different cultures by role-playing in small groups the following situations:

1. An American party like the one described in Questionnaire 2.
2. A party given by someone from your culture, attended by an American who tries to be a polite guest according to the customs of American culture.
3. A party given by an American, attended by someone from your culture who tries to be a polite guest according to the customs of your culture.

ADDITIONAL INTERVIEWS

1.   Changes in American customs   Are American social customs the same today as they were in the past? Using the questions on Questionnaire 2, interview an older American about what it was like in the past. At the beginning of the interview, explain to the American you are interviewing: "Imagine that you are attending a party during the time when your parents (or your grandparents) were young. How long ago was that? Answer the questions according to what people thought was the polite way to act back then." After your interview, compare the answers with your first interview with an American and decide what customs have changed in modern American society.

2.   What your clothes say about you   Every culture gives special meaning to clothing. For example, in the United States, brides wear white, the color of purity, while in China, brides are married in red, the color of good luck. Find out what an American thinks is correct and incorrect clothing for different situations. Ask questions like, "What do Americans wear to a formal wedding? How can you tell if someone has good or bad taste from their clothes?"

3.   More on politeness and respect   Ask an American how politeness and respect are shown in different situations, for example: when you talk to a clerk at a store, when you answer the telephone, when you go to a home for dinner, when you ask your boss for some time off, when you meet your professor on the street.

4.   Table manners   First, think about the table manners in your own culture. For example, what things did your parents teach you *never* to do at the table? What did they teach you *always* to do when eating? Make a list. Then interview an American about the table manners he or she was taught as a child, asking the two questions above. Discuss your list with the American and ask how many of the table manners from your culture are the same as those in the United States.

In Conclusion

When you see an American acting in an impolite way, how can you tell if it is because of cultural differences or because of rudeness? Sometimes it is difficult to know, but it is a question you must always ask yourself. Think over your experiences, and give two examples. First, describe a situation where an American acted impolitely by the customs of your culture, but not by American customs. Then describe a situation where an American acted impolitely by American customs.

Chapter 5

Family Patterns

A nuclear family

If you ask someone ,"Do you come from a large family?" do you mean brothers and sisters, or cousins, aunts, and uncles as well?

Preparation

PREREADING VOCABULARY EXERCISE

Study the sentences below. The words in *italics* are defined in parentheses.

> *child rearing — crisis — extended family — family pattern — interdependence — to make it on one's own — nuclear family — responsible, responsibility — to take advantage of —*

1. In many cultures, grandparents help a lot with *child rearing.* (bringing up children)
2. Grandparents, cousins, aunts, and uncles also help out in times of *crisis.* (serious problems)
3. To Hispanics and Asians the *extended family* is more important than it is to Americans. (grandparents, cousins, aunts, and uncles)

An extended family

4. This chapter is about *family patterns*. (who is in the family and how they act with each other)

5. In many Hispanic and Asian cultures, families are built around the value of *interdependence*. (cooperation, depending on each other for help)

6. In the United States the person who can *make it on his own* is respected. (succeed without help from others)

7. In American culture the *nuclear family* is more important than other family members. (parents and children)

8. Rosa had always seemed like such an independent, *responsible* person, who never missed a class. (always doing what one must do)

9. Most Americans would feel little *responsibility* toward their second cousins. (duty, obligation, the feeling that one should take care of someone)

10. "It's not fair of your cousin *to take advantage of* you." (to use unfairly)

Directions

In each numbered sentence below, fill in the blank with the best word from the above vocabulary list. Change tense and number (singular and plural) where necessary.

Example A. When I was growing up, I did not often see my *extended family* because we lived far from my uncles and aunts.

1. The _____ is more common in many cultures than is the nuclear family.

2. Grandparents help pass on the traditions to their grandchildren; therefore, children whose only contact is with their _____ may not know much about their family's past.

3. It is easy to _____ a generous person.

4. In extended families, taking care of the older people is usually the _____ of sons and daughters, and sometimes of nieces and nephews.

5. In extended families, grandparents often have the responsibility of _____ .

CASE STUDY

Rosa and Annie shared a small dormitory room at a university. Annie was American and Rosa was Mexican-American. They liked each other very much and got along well until a problem came up.

One day, Rosa told Annie, "My second cousin wants to come see the university. She might want to go to school here next year. Do you mind if she stays with us while she visits?"

Annie answered, "Gee, it's pretty crowded with just the two of us. Where's she going to sleep?"

"Oh, that's no problem. She can sleep in my bed, with me."

"Well, okay," said Annie. "It's up to you."

"Great!" answered Rosa. "She's coming tomorrow."

Two weeks later, the cousin was still with them. Since she did not bring enough money, Rosa paid for all her meals. Rosa missed many of her classes so that she could help her cousin find her way around.

Rosa never complained about any of this to Annie, but Annie decided to speak to her friend.

"Rosa," she said. "I know it's none of my business. But I don't like to see you being treated this way. It's not fair of your cousin to take advantage of you, using your time and your money like this. And how do you ever get any sleep, anyway? I think you should tell her you have your own life to live. After all, she's only your second cousin."

Rosa was surprised. She answered, "Oh, the bed doesn't bother me! It reminds me of sleeping with my sister as a child. You're right, though, about my schoolwork. I know I'm missing too many classes. But family comes first. I just couldn't leave my cousin here by herself."

Even after their conversation, Annie still could not understand her friend. Before her cousin arrived, Rosa had always seemed like such an independent, responsible person, who never missed a class. Annie just could not understand why she had changed.

Questions

1. Why was Annie confused?
2. Why did Rosa continue to help her cousin?
3. Do you think Rosa's and Annie's ideas are typical of their cultures?
4. Would you do the same for your second cousin as Rosa did?

BACKGROUND

One of the reasons that Annie could not understand Rosa is this: in American culture, the nuclear family is much more important to the individual than the extended family. Most Americans feel little responsibility toward their second cousins, and may never even have met them. Therefore, Annie was confused because Rosa put so much effort into helping "just" a second cousin. But in Rosa's culture there is not such a big difference between nuclear and extended family responsibilities. For many Hispanics, Asians, Africans, and Arabs, the extended family is very important in child rearing, in social life, and in caring for older people. In these societies, the extended family is the main financial and emotional support for people in times of crisis. This is not so for most Americans, who rely more on friends, institutions, and professionals.

Another reason why Annie and Rosa could not understand each other is different cultural values. Rosa felt that "family comes first," which means that her own needs come second. Annie had a hard time understanding that point of view because in her culture the individual usually comes first. In the United States the person who can "make it on his own" without help from family is respected, although of course many people do get help from their families. For Americans, it is very important for the individual to be independent of others, and this value is true in American family life too. In Hispanic and Asian cultures, family members depend on each other more, and families are built around the value of interdependence.

Because of these differences, it is sometimes difficult for people to understand and accept the way family members in other cultures seem to treat each other. People from Latin America and Asia may feel that American families are cold and distant because of the independence of family members. Americans may feel that close extended families in other cultures ask too much from their members and make them too dependent. It is important to remember that families show their love in very different ways. These differences sometimes make it hard to see the reality of family love in every culture in the world.

PREINTERVIEW VOCABULARY EXERCISE

argue — babysitter — discipline — godparent — household — relative

Directions

Study the sentences below. The words in *italics* are defined in parentheses.

1. Do all teenagers *argue* with their parents? (disagree openly)
2. Do parents leave their children with *babysitters*? (someone paid to take care of children, not a family member)
3. Who in your family *disciplined* the children? (made them behave)
4. Did your *godparent* discipline you? (when a child is baptized in some Christian churches one or two adults are chosen by the parents to have a special relationship to the child.)
5. Who lives in your *household*? (the people who live in a house or apartment together)
6. When you have a problem, do you usually get help from a friend or from a *relative*? (family member)

Directions

In the numbered sentences below, fill in the blanks with the words in italics from the sentences above which fit the meaning best. Change tense and number (singular and plural) where necessary.

1. Many American teenagers work as _____ to earn extra money and

   to learn about children.

2. Often Americans pay a _____ , such as the child's aunt, to babysit.

3. The methods that parents use to _____ their children vary from culture to culture.

4. Although the nuclear family is still common in the United States, more and more _____ fit other patterns, such as single parent families and people living alone.

5. In some families when the parents die, the children are then raised by their _____ .

Interviews and Analysis

• QUESTIONNAIRE 1 •
FAMILY PATTERNS AND VALUES

Directions

Answer the following questions yourself, according to the way your family raised you. Or use the questionnaire to interview a classmate from another culture.

1. In your family, who gave you your names? How were your names chosen?

2. When you were a child, who took care of you when your parents were not home?

3. When you were a child, whom did you sleep with?

4. When you were growing up, who lived in your household?

5. In your household, when you were growing up, what were the children's responsibilities?

6. When you were a child, which did your parents try harder to teach you—independence or cooperation?

7. In your culture, what do people think of a young person of 18, not married, who moves out from his or her parents' home?

8. What do people think of a 27-year-old person who lives at home with his or her parents?

9. Nowadays, when you have a problem, do you usually go to a friend or to a relative for help? Explain.

10. In your culture, when people get old, where do they live, and what money do they live on?

Name: _____ Culture: _____

● QUESTIONNAIRE 2 ●
AMERICAN FAMILY STRUCTURE AND VALUES

Interview an American about his or her family structure and values, using the following questionnaire. Make up one question of your own, and write any new vocabulary at the end of the questionnaire.

1. In your family, who gave you your names? How were your names chosen?

2. When you were a child, who took care of you when your parents were not home?

3. When you were a child, whom did you sleep with?

4. When you were growing up, who lived in your household?

5. What were the children's responsibilities in your household?

6. When you were a child, which did your parents try harder to teach you—independence or cooperation?

7. In the United States, what do people think of a young person of 18, not married, who moves out from his or her parents' home?

8. What do people think of a 27-year-old person who lives at home with his or her parents?

9. Nowadays, when you have a problem, do you usually go to a friend or to a relative for help? Explain.

10. In the United States, when people get old, where do they live, and what money do they live on?

11. (Your own question)

Person interviewed: _____ Sex: _____

Age (more or less): _____ Ethnic background: _____

Father's work: _____

New vocabulary

INDIVIDUAL ANALYSIS

1. Compare the answers that you wrote down on Questionnaires 1 and 2. On which questions are the answers similar?

2. On which questions are they different?

3. Can you explain the differences?

4. Which answer given by an American surprised you the most? Why?

GROUP ANALYSIS

In class, compare the answers to Questionnaire 2 given by all the Americans interviewed by the class. Write down the most common American answer to each question and also some of the other answers that only some of the Americans gave.

Most common American answer	Other answers
1.	
2.	
3.	
4.	
5.	
6.	
7.	
8.	
9.	
10.	

Questions

1. Which of the common American answers are examples of the importance of the nuclear family in American family life?

2. Which of the common American answers are examples of the value of independence in American family life?

3. Discuss the answers to the questions that members of the class made up themselves (question 11).

4. Look over the "other answers" given by Americans listed above. Some of the Americans' answers may be explained by their age, sex, social class, or ethnic background. For example, it is more common for American young people from working-class homes to live at home until marriage than it is for children in middle- or upper-class families. Can you explain some of the different answers given by Americans by their age, sex, social class, or ethnic background?

Additional Activities

ADDITIONAL INTERVIEW

Find out about American family celebrations such as weddings, christenings, or even funerals. Write your own list of questions to ask an American. Include details such as gifts, food, dress, and guests. Write up all the information or present it orally in class.

ROLE PLAY

Role-play the conflict between Annie and Rosa. Then consider the following family situations and, in a small group, choose one to act out. Perform it two ways: as it would happen in an American family and as it would happen in a family from another culture.

1. Son or daughter graduates from college and has a conflict with parents over where to live.
2. Grandmother dies and the family discusses what will happen to grandfather.
3. Mother of three small children receives a phone call that her sister, in another city, is very ill. What does she do?
4. The school calls the parents to report that their teenaged child was caught smoking marijuana.

WRITING ASSIGNMENT

How has family life in your culture changed in recent years? Write a paragraph that begins with the sentence, "There have been several changes in _____ families since my grandparents were children."

In Conclusion

Think over all that you have learned about American family patterns and values. What do you think are the biggest changes in family life for a family from your country that moves to the United States? What are the main problems or conflicts that a family faces?

Chapter 6

Male/Female Roles

A little girl playing with her toy trucks.

In the last 15 years, many Americans have started to think that little girls will grow up to be happier and healthier if they are free to explore all their interests. When you were a child, was there anything that you were told *not* to do or play with because you were a girl or a boy?

Preparation

PREREADING VOCABULARY EXERCISE

Study the sentences below. The words in *italics* are defined in parentheses.

assumption — chance — chaperone — owe — partner — reality — roles

1. Blanca's understanding that Kevin was going to pay for her is an example of a cultural *assumption*. (a belief that something is true)
2. "Men will always try to make love to a woman whenever they have the *chance*." (opportunity, possibility)
3. Blanca's parents sent a *chaperone* with her on a date. (someone who goes out with two unmarried people so that they are not alone together)
4. Some women say that if a man pays for them, they feel as if they *owe* him something. (the feeling that one should give someone something)
5. Some women like to feel like an equal *partner* on a date. (a person who shares something with another as an equal)
6. A cultural assumption is a way to understand *reality*. (what is real or true)
7. Women's and men's *roles* are changing very fast. (how a person is supposed to act; a person's responsibilities)

Directions

In each numbered sentence, fill in the blank with the best word from the above vocabulary list. Change tense and number (singular and plural) where necessary.

1. Some people think that this is the first time in American history that

   women have the same _____ to get ahead as men.

2. In the past, men's and women's _____ were very different, so

   women almost never worked the same jobs as men.

3. Today, the fact that women work in almost every kind of job and

   profession in America is a _____ , whether people like it or not.

4. However, women are not equal yet; for example, there are very few big

   businesses where the _____ who own them are women.

5. Many American bosses still prefer to give a job to a man because of their

_____ that women workers will leave the company as soon as they

get married or have a baby.

CASE STUDY

Kevin was leaving work one Friday, when he stopped to talk to Blanca, a new worker. On Wednesday, they had talked at lunch. She had told him that she had just come from the Dominican Republic two months before. Kevin liked her.

"So, Blanca, what are your plans for the weekend?" asked Kevin.

"Oh, hi Kevin," Blanca smiled. "I have to go shopping with my cousin for a winter coat."

"Tonight some of us from work are going out to a place called 'The Blue Hat' for beers and something to eat. Would you like to come? I could pick you up at eight if you tell me where you live."

"Okay, Kevin. That sounds nice. I hope it's O.K. if I bring my little sister along."

"As your chaperone?" laughed Kevin, making a joke.

"That's right," said Blanca. "I guess you know something about Dominican culture. It's the only way my parents will let me go."

"Are you serious?" Kevin stared at her. "Well, I'll be there at eight."

When Kevin, Blanca, and her sister arrived at "The Blue Hat," they sat down with Kevin's friends, who were already eating. A waiter came and asked, "What would you like to have? And shall I put this all on one check or will you all pay separately?"

"Separate checks, please," answered Kevin. "I'll have a hamburger and French fries and a beer, please. Blanca?"

Blanca opened her purse under the table. Then she whispered something to her sister in Spanish. She looked at the waiter and said, "My sister and I aren't hungry. A coke and a beer, please."

Questions

1. Why did Blanca bring along her little sister?
2. Why was Kevin surprised?
3. Why did Kevin say, "Separate checks, please"?
4. Why did Blanca say she wasn't hungry?

BACKGROUND

Blanca thought that Kevin was going to pay for her because he had invited her to go out. Until recently, this was the American custom, as well. But things are changing. One reason is that many more American women work today. So, many men and women think it is unfair for men to always pay for everything when they go out. Another reason is that some women say that if a man pays for them, they feel like they owe him something. And some American women prefer to pay because they like to feel like an equal partner on a date. They don't feel equal if they are taken places and paid for.

But lots of American men still do pay for women on dates. They feel it is the man's role to do so. Many American women agree. With women's and men's roles changing so fast in the United States, it is often confusing to know what to do, even for Americans.

Blanca's understanding that Kevin was going to pay for her is an example of a cultural assumption. A cultural assumption is a belief about the way the world works, a way to understand reality. It is shared by the people of a culture. Our cultural assumptions are so much a part of us that many times we cannot believe that the whole world does not see things as we do. But trying to understand cultural assumptions other people make can help explain their way of thinking and acting.

For example, Kevin was surprised, maybe even shocked, that Blanca's parents sent a chaperone with her on a date. American parents assume young people will never learn to act responsibly unless they are given some responsibility and independence. Because of this, American parents allow their unmarried children to go out alone on dates after they reach a certain age. It is not that they don't care about their children. Rather, American parents feel their children must learn to become independent. Kevin was surprised about the chaperone because to the American way of thinking, Blanca's parents were treating her like a child.

What are the Hispanic cultural assumptions? Most Hispanic parents assume the worst will happen if they let their daughters go out alone with a man. "Men will always try to make love to a woman whenever they have the chance" is a Latin cultural assumption about men. And the Hispanic assumption about women is that they will not be able to stop a man. Because of these assumptions about men and women, most Hispanic parents feel that it is their responsibility to make sure that their daughters are not left alone on a date.

PREINTERVIEW VOCABULARY EXERCISE

Study the sentences below. The words in *italics* are defined in parentheses.

> *bride — couple — engagement — maternity leave — opinion —
> pressure — promotion — support — traditional*

1. Does the *bride* take her husband's name? (a woman getting married)
2. Is it common for a *couple* who are not married to live together? (two people connected in some way, usually a man and a woman)
3. How long does a typical *engagement* last? (the time between the decision to get married and the wedding.)

4. When working women have babies, they get a paid *maternity leave*. (time off from a job)

5. What is your *opinion* about marriage? (what someone thinks about something)

6. Is there *pressure* on a couple to have a baby? (other people wanting someone or telling someone to do something)

7. If a man and a woman apply for the same job or *promotion*, are the chances better for the man? (a better job in the same place of work)

8. What are the *traditional* careers or jobs for women in the United States? (typical or usual in the past)

9. Are there many women in the United States who are heads of households, that is, who must *support* their children by themselves? (pay for whatever someone needs)

Directions

In each numbered sentence, fill in the blank with the best word from the vocabulary list. Change tense and singular and plural where necessary.

1. Fifty years ago, many things were different for American _____

   planning to get married.

2. First of all, it was common for an _____ to last years; today, most

   people don't wait that long.

3. One reason people had to wait so long was that 50 years ago, only the

   husband _____ the family; today, of course, many more wives

   work too.

4. In the past, a couple who wanted to marry sometimes had to wait years for

   the man to get a _____ so that they would have enough money to

   live on.

5. Longer engagements may result in fewer divorces, in the _____ of

   some people.

Interviews and Analysis

INTERVIEW INSTRUCTIONS

The subject of male/female roles is so large and complicated that in this chapter you will be able to choose one of three questionnaires to use for your interview with an American. The topics covered by each questionnaire are: Questionnaire 1: Male/Female Roles in the American Family; Questionnaire 2: Male/Female Roles in the American Workplace; Questionnaire 3: American Dating and Marriage Customs. As in other chapters, you should make up a question of your own and write down the new vocabulary you learned during the interview.

After your interview, in the Individual Analysis section compare the American's answers with the most common customs and attitudes in your culture. Then, compare your interview with those of your classmates who used the same questionnaire. Present a report to the class.

• QUESTIONNAIRE 1 •
MALE/FEMALE ROLES IN THE AMERICAN FAMILY

1. Do most American couples hope for sons or daughters? What is your own opinion?

2. Do most American parents expect little girls to act differently from little boys? If so, in what ways? What is your own opinion?

3. In most American families, are sisters expected to do what their brothers tell them to do? What is your own opinion?

4. In most American families, do the sons and daughters do the same kinds of jobs around the house? Please explain. What do you think about this?

5. In most American families, do husbands and wives share the housework? What do you think about this?

6. How much do American fathers help take care of the children? How do you feel about this?

7. Will most American parents pay as much for a son's education as for a daughter's? Do they think it is as important for their daughters to finish their education as for their sons? What do you think about this?

8. How do most American husbands feel about their wives working? Do you agree?

9. Is it against the law in the United States for a husband to hit his wife? Is it common for a husband to hit his wife?

10. In a typical American marriage, what happens if the wife wants to do something her husband doesn't want her to do? What do you think a couple should do in that situation?

11. In most American families, who pays the family's bills and takes care of money matters? What about your family?

12. When parents die, do they usually leave the same amount of money to their daughters as to their sons?

13. (Your own question)

Person interviewed: _____ Sex: _____

Age: _____ Ethnic background: _____

New vocabulary

• QUESTIONNAIRE 2 •
MALE/FEMALE ROLES IN THE AMERICAN WORKPLACE

1. What are the traditional careers or jobs for women in the United States?

2. What are the traditional jobs or careers that are for men only?

3. In the United States do men and women always get the same pay if they do the same job? Please explain. Are there any laws about this?

4. Do you think there are any jobs that women can't do as well as men? Do you think there are any jobs that men can't do as well as women?

5. If a man and a woman apply for the same job or promotion, are the chances better for the man? Are there any laws about this?

6. Do most American women continue to work when they get married? Why or why not?

7. Do most of the women that you know who have children have a paid job as well? What do you think about this?

8. Did your mother have a job while you were growing up? Did most women your mother's age work? Why or why not?

9. When working women have babies, do they get a paid maternity leave? How much time do they usually take off from work after a baby is born? Is there such a thing as a paternity leave?

10. Are there many women in the United States who are heads of households, that is, who must support their children by themselves? Does the government help these women at all?

11. In the jobs you have held, have males and females had the same opportunities? Please explain.

12. (Your own question)

Person interviewed: _____ Sex: _____

Age: _____ Ethnic background: _____

New vocabulary

• QUESTIONNAIRE 3 •
AMERICAN DATING AND MARRIAGE CUSTOMS

1. At what age do Americans today usually start dating?

2. Based on your experience, describe a typical date.

3. Who invites whom and who pays on a typical date today?

4. Do parents have anything to say about their children's dating? Until what age?

5. Is it common for a man and woman who are not married to live together? Is it accepted?

6. When a man and woman want to get married, do they usually ask their parents or tell them? Is it a problem if a son or daughter wants to marry someone outside his or her religion, race, or ethnic group?

7. How long does a typical engagement last?

8. At about what age do most people you know marry? Why?

9. Describe some traditional American marriage customs, such as the bridal shower, the rings, the honeymoon.

10. Who usually pays for the wedding itself? The rings? The furniture and the other household items for the couple's new home?

11. Does the bride always take her husband's name? Explain.

12. Do most couples today have children soon after marriage? Is there pressure on them to do so? What happens if a couple cannot have children?

13. Is divorce common in the United States today? What do you think the reasons for it are? Is it accepted?

14. Do you know any women who have had children without being married? Is this accepted?

15. (Your own question)

Person interviewed: _____ Sex: _____

Age: _____ Ethnic background: _____

New vocabulary

INDIVIDUAL ANALYSIS

Compare the answers you received on the questionnaire with the way you would answer the same questions about your culture. What are the main similarities and the main differences between American customs and attitudes and those in your culture?

GROUP ANALYSIS

Meet with others in your class who interviewed Americans using the same questionnaire (of the three choices) that you did. Compare the answers that you received and discuss the following questions. Based on the group's answers, prepare a report in oral or written form.

Questions

1. What was the most common answer to each of the questions; that is, how did most of the Americans answer?

2. Write a list of some American cultural assumptions that might explain these answers.
    For example, what if most Americans answered "no" to the question, "In most American families, are sisters expected to do what their brothers tell them to do?" This answer could be explained by two American cultural assumptions. One assumption is that in many American families brothers and sisters do not usually have responsibility for taking care of each other. Another assumption is that age is more important than sex, so that in an American family, an older sister would never have to do what her younger brother told her to do.

3. Were there some questions for which there were a lot of different answers or for which there seemed to be a lot of conflicting opinions among the people interviewed? To which questions did people interviewed have the most different answers?

4. Looking over some of the differences mentioned in question 3 above, can you tell if the age, sex, or ethnic background of the people interviewed could help explain some of their answers? For example, if some people answered "yes" and others answered "no" to the question, "Do American men and women share the housework?" did men answer one way and women the other?

5. Does it seem as if men's and women's roles are changing in the United States today? Give some examples from your interview.

6. What are some of the biggest differences between the American customs and attitudes and those of other cultures represented in your group?

Additional Activities

ADDITIONAL INTERVIEW

Asking the same questions, interview an American of the opposite sex from the American you already interviewed for this chapter. How do the two sets of answers differ? Or write your own questionnaire about some aspect of male/female roles in American society past, present, or future, and interview an American.

DEBATES

In small groups, choose one issue concerning male/female roles such as: (1) the government should/should not prohibit sex discrimination on the job, or (2) a working mother helps/hurts her children's development. Divide into teams to debate the issue before the class. The class should judge each team on logic, facts, and presentation.

ROLE PLAY

Imagine some possible misunderstandings between people of two cultural groups due to differences in male/female roles. Then:

1. Role-play one misunderstanding.
2. Role-play the same situation, but where the misunderstanding is resolved in some way.
3. Role-play the situation in which all the people are American.
4. Role-play the situation in which all the people are from a non-American cultural group.

GUEST SPEAKER

Invite a speaker from a women's organization such as NOW (the National Organization for Women) or a campus women's group to speak to the class. Prepare questions such as: Have American women progressed in recent years? What does your organization think are the most important issues facing women in the United States today?

In Conclusion

Your own ideas about men's and women's roles may be a mixture or combination of the ideas from your own culture and American ideas on the subject. How have your own opinions about men's and women's roles changed since you have had contact with Americans? What do you think is positive about your own culture's attitudes, customs, and assumptions about men and women? What do you think is negative? What is positive about the American attitudes, customs, and assumptions? What is negative?

Chapter 7

Is Your Time
My Time ?

What have you noticed about Americans' attitudes toward time?

Preparation

PREREADING VOCABULARY EXERCISE

Study the sentences below. The words in *italics* are defined in parentheses.

> *accomplish — concept — exchange program — flexible — goal —*
> *maturity — morally — orientation — rush — schedule — sin*

1. Many Americans believe that time should be used to *accomplish* certain goals. (do; finish)

2. In many ways, Martha's *concept* of time is typically American. (idea of, attitude toward; the way someone understands something)

3. She was chosen to spend a summer in Indonesia as part of a student *exchange program*. (people from different countries changing places and spending time living with each other's families)

4. A more *flexible* concept of time is more common in agricultural societies, where nature, not the clock, sets the time for people to work. (able to bend or change; not fixed or rigid)

5. Martha's *goal* was to experience everything she could. (what someone wants to or plans to do)

6. In the American way of thinking, new is better than old, just as youth is valued more than *maturity*. (adulthood; the time of life after youth)

7. The Puritans believed strongly in the "work ethic," the idea that work is *morally* good. (for the spirit or the soul)

8. The United States is future-*oriented*, or has a future *orientation*. (has more interest in the future than in the past or present)

9. "Doesn't it bother you to *rush* around so much?" (hurry)

10. She did not even feel a bit sad about leaving behind her busy *schedule* back home: her piano lessons, the diving team, her church youth group, and her baby-sitting job. (planned things to do)

11. The Puritans believed that it is a *sin* to be doing nothing. (an act against one's religion, against the will of God)

Directions

In each numbered sentence below, fill in the blank with the best word from the vocabulary list above. Change tense and number (singular and plural) where necessary.

1. Thousands of high school students each year leave their homes to live with a family in another country. Some participate in programs run by the American Field Service, known as AFS, a large student _____ .

2. To improve international understanding is one of the main _____ of AFS.

3. Most AFS students who have returned home agree that this goal is usually _____ on a personal level at least.

4. One reason the program works so well is that young people are so much more _____ than older people.

5. AFS's assumption is that if teenagers learn to understand another culture's way of seeing things, that lesson will stay with them throughout their _____ as well.

CASE STUDY

Martha was an American high school student who was chosen to spend a summer in Indonesia as part of a student exchange program. When she got her letter of acceptance, she felt very lucky. She was sure it was going to be the most exciting experience of her life. She did not even feel a bit sad about leaving behind her busy schedule back home: her piano lessons, the diving team, her church youth group, and her baby-sitting job.

The first few days after her arrival in Indonesia were filled with meeting her new Indonesian exchange family, trying new foods, walking around the neighborhood, and getting to know her Indonesian exchange sister, Ketty. It was just as exciting as Martha had hoped. But about her second week in Indonesia, Martha began to feel as if something was wrong.

One morning, after breakfast, she looked at her watch and asked Ketty, "So, what are the plans for today? What are we going to do?"

Ketty replied, "Oh, I didn't really make any plans. My mother might want us to go shopping with her later. Then we'll see what we feel like doing. Maybe we could go downtown."

Martha answered, "What time is your mom going shopping?"

"Oh, whenever she's ready. Are you getting bored, Martha? Maybe we should sign up for one of those guided tours of the city. The downtown hotels have them for American tourists. Would you like that?"

"Oh, no, I don't want to be a tourist. I want to do just what you do. I guess I'm just used to being busy all the time. It's hard for me to get used to not having plans," said Martha.

"Doesn't it bother you to rush around so much?" asked Ketty.

"No, I love it when I'm busy. Sitting around wasting time makes me nervous. Let's go do something, Ketty. I'm only here for two months, after all. I don't want to leave Indonesia feeling that I haven't experienced as much as I can." Martha looked down at her watch again and said, "Goodness, it's almost 11 and all we've done is sit around talking!"

Questions

1. What was Martha's life like at home?
2. Why did she begin to feel as if something was wrong?
3. What can you tell about the Indonesian concept of time?
4. What can you tell about Martha's concept of time?
5. What could make Martha feel better again?

BACKGROUND

In many ways, Martha's concept of time is typically American. She worried about "wasting" her time in Indonesia if every minute was not planned. It was hard for her to be happy if she wasn't busy doing something. Many Americans believe that time should be "used wisely" as much as possible, that is, used to accomplish certain goals. In Martha's case, her goal was to experience everything she could. To her, experiencing Indonesia meant running around doing many things. She may have missed some important experiences of Indonesian life because she could not slow down and relax.

It is easier to understand how people think about time by using some concepts from anthropology, the study of different cultures. Anthropologists ask: Which is more important to each culture: the future, the present, or the past? Most Americans act as if they think that the future is most important: the United States is future-oriented. Part of the American orientation toward the future is the value placed on accomplishing goals. Americans rush through the present in order to accomplish some goal for the future. Another example of Americans' orientation toward the future is the way change is valued. In the American way of thinking, new is better than old, just as youth is valued more than maturity. Other cultures are more oriented toward the present or toward the past. For example, Ketty's idea of waiting until later to "see what we feel like doing" shows a present orientation. In Chinese culture, which is past-oriented, tradition and old age are both respected.

Although Martha's goal was to "experience" as much as she could in Indonesia, she didn't seem to think "sitting around" was an important experience. That is because Americans value doing, or action, more than simply being. They are "action-oriented," not "being-oriented." Why do so many Americans feel they must be busy to be happy? Perhaps the idea comes from the Protestant religion of the Puritans, the first English people to live in America. The Puritans believed strongly in the "work ethic," the idea that work is morally good. The Puritans believed doing nothing was a sin. These ideas may help explain how uncomfortable many modern Americans feel about "wasting time."

To avoid wasting time, Americans plan their time as much as possible, and measure it carefully. In the case study, Martha looked at her watch twice, even though she had no worry of being late. She felt uncomfortable without a planned schedule of things to do, as she had back home. Many busy Americans carry a small calendar around with them, to help them remember their daily schedule. They only see friends when they have made an appointment to do so.

In other cultures, the concept of time is more flexible. Things happen when they are ready to happen, rather than when the clock says so. People see their friends when they feel like getting together, not when their calendar or watch tells them it is time. This more flexible concept of time is common in agricultural rather than industrialized cultures. There, it is nature, not the clock, that sets the schedule by which people work. In contrast, the modern factory system of urban, industrialized societies may have forced people to become slaves to the clock.

Interviews and Analysis

•QUESTIONNAIRE 1•
THE MEANINGS OF TIME

Directions

Answer the following questions yourself, according to the typical customs of your culture. Or, use the questionnaire to interview a classmate from another culture.

1. If you planned a dinner party, when would you tell your guests about it?

2. If you planned on serving dinner at 8:00, at what time would you ask your guests to arrive? _____ How would you feel if someone came at 9:00?

3. If you yourself were invited to a dinner party for 8:00, at what time would you probably arrive? _____ Why?

4. If you were invited to a big dance that began at 8:00, at what time would you probably arrive? _____ Why?

5. Imagine that a good friend promised to meet you at a local coffee shop at a certain time but was late. After how long would you begin

to worry that your friend was not coming at all? _____
How would you feel about your friend being late?

6. Imagine that you promised to pick up a friend at a certain time to go shopping, but you arrived late. When would you feel that you had to say you were sorry—after how many minutes (or hours) late? _____ What would you say?

7. If you had a dentist's appointment for 4:00, at what time would you probably arrive? _____ What would happen if you arrived late? In your native country, do dentists schedule appointments for specific times, the way they do in the United States?

8. If you had a job interview at 9:00, at what time would you probably arrive? _____ What would happen if you arrived late?

9. Do you think that your answers to these questions are typical of the way most people from your culture would answer? Please explain.

10. How do you feel about someone who is always late?

11. How do you feel about someone who is always in a hurry?

12. In your culture, what time of life do people think is the best: childhood, youth, middle age, or old age? Why?

13. In your culture, which time of life do people think is the worst? Why?

Name: _____ Culture: _____

• QUESTIONNAIRE 2 •
THE MEANINGS OF TIME TO AN AMERICAN

Directions

Interview an American and ask him or her to answer the following questions. Ask a question of your own, related to the topic. At the end, write down any new vocabulary that you learned or heard in the interview.

1. If you were planning a dinner party, when would you tell your guests about it?

2. If you planned on serving dinner at 8:00, at what time would you ask your guests to arrive? _____ How would you feel if someone came at 9:00?

3. If you yourself were invited to a dinner party for 8:00, at what time would you probably arrive? _____ Why?

4. If you were invited to a big dance that began at 8:00, at what time would you probably arrive? _____ Why?

5. Imagine that a good friend promised to meet you at a coffee shop at a certain time but was late. After how long would you begin to worry that your friend was not coming at all? _____ How would you feel about your friend being late?

6. Imagine that you promised to pick up a friend at a certain time to go shopping, but you arrived late. When would you feel that you had to say you were sorry—after how many minutes (or hours) late? _____ What would you say?

7. If you had a dentist's appointment for 4:00, at what time would you probably arrive? _____ What would happen if you arrived late?

8. If you had a job interview at 9:00, at what time would you probably arrive? _____ What would happen if you arrived late?

9. Do you think that your answers to these questions are typical of the way most Americans would answer? Please explain.

10. How do you feel about someone who is always late?

11. How do you feel about someone who is always in a hurry?

12. What time of life do most Americans think is the best: childhood, youth, middle age, or old age? Why?

13. Which time of life do people think is the worst? Why?

14. (Your own question)

Person interviewed: _____

New vocabulary

INDIVIDUAL ANALYSIS

Think about the answers that you would give to the questions on the questionnaire, and compare them with the answers given by the American you interviewed. Then answer:

1. Which questions would you answer the same as the American did?

2. Which questions would you answer differently?

3. Are any of the American's answers examples of the American orientation toward the future (see Background)? Explain.

4. Do you think that your culture is more oriented toward the past, present, or future? Explain or give examples.

GROUP ANALYSIS

Compare the answers given by all the Americans interviewed by the class, and answer these questions.

1. For questions 2 through 8, what was the average time given? (Note: to find out the average time for each question, add up all the times and divide by the number of questionnaires):

   (2) _____ (3) _____ (4) _____ (5) _____ (6) _____ (7) _____

   (8) _____

2. Do Americans think it is equally important to be on time for social occasions (questions 2 to 6) as to be prompt for business occasions (questions 7, 8)?

3. What do Americans think of people who are late?

4. Did the interviews with Americans show any examples of Americans' orientation toward the future?

5. Did all the Americans interviewed give the same answers to all the questions? If not, what were some of the differences?

Additional Activities

LANGUAGE STUDY

Find some proverbs in English relating to time, such as the American "Early to bed, early to rise, makes a man healthy, wealthy, and wise." Also make a list of English expressions used in relation to time, such as "to budget time" and "to lose time." Translate from your native language expressions and proverbs related to time as well. Analyze both the English and native language expressions to see how they show the cultural meanings given to time. For example, the native American Sioux language does not have any words at all to express the concept "late" because in that culture time represents something controlled by nature, not by man. On the other hand, the expression "waste time" reflects the American concept that time can be controlled, and that it is something valuable.

ETHNOGRAPHIC OBSERVATION

Another aspect of time which varies from culture to culture is the way that we order our activities. Some individuals, and some cultures (such as German, English, and American) are *monochronic,* which means that they do things one thing at a time. Monochronic people like to finish one thing before starting another, and they do not like to be interrupted. For example, American customers wait in lines at stores, so that the sales clerk can finish helping each one before going on to the next. Other people are *polychronic,* because they are able to do several different things at once and to pay attention to more than one thing at a time. In Latin America, a polychronic culture, sales clerks wait on several customers at once. *Monochronism* or *polychronism* can be seen in different activities, such as in conversation (group conversations or talking in pairs) or in ways of doing business.

Some people think that more Americans are monochronic and that things are set up for people to do one thing at a time. It is easy to observe American monochronism in any store, bank, or post office. Spend at least 10 minutes watching the clerks in one of these settings wait on the customers. Observe their interaction, especially the nonverbal communication. Try to notice:

1. Is there a clear line, or a group around the counter?

2. How do customers in the line deal with other customers who ignore the line or try to cut in?

3. Do the clerks deal with several customers at a time, or one by one?

4. How does the clerk signal that he or she is ready to attend to a customer (both verbally and nonverbally)?

5. How do the customers get the attention of the clerk?

6. What conversation takes place besides the business at hand?

Make a summary of the results of your observation. Then compare what you observed with the way a similar situation would take place in your native culture. Is your culture more monochronic or polychronic, in your opinion? Can you give any other examples?

ROLE PLAY

Read over the section above on monochronism and polychronism. Role-play any of the situations below two ways: as it would happen in a monochronic culture, and as it would happen in a polychronic culture.

Situations

1. Customers at a record store (customers wait in line versus salesperson waiting on several at once)

2. A second-grade class discussion about students' summer vacations (raising hands, taking turns versus students talking without raising hands)

3. A welcoming reception for students given by a college (people breaking off to talk in pairs versus larger group conversations)

In Conclusion

In your opinion, what are some of the positive things about the American attitude toward time? What are some of the negative things?

Chapter 8

Money Talks, But What Does It Say?

Would you ever ask a friend how much she paid for her new outfit? If not, why not? Do you think that your feelings about this are cultural?

Preparation

PREREADING VOCABULARY EXERCISE

Study the sentences below. The words in *italics* are defined in parentheses.

> *appreciated — borrow — debt — favor — insist — lend —*
> *obligation — owe — refusal — rely/self-reliance — trust*

1. I really *appreciated* this last night. (was grateful, was thankful, was glad for)

2. I needed to *borrow* money. (to take something with the idea of giving it back later)

3. Americans cannot respect themselves if they feel too much *"in debt"* to other people. (a *debt* is an amount of money that someone has borrowed and must return; *in debt* is the feeling that you must give someone something back)

4. I need a *favor*. (something that someone does for someone else, without getting paid)

5. I *insist* on paying you back your money. (refuse to take no for an answer)

6. "Could you *lend* me a dollar?" (give something with the understanding that it will be returned)

7. Americans prefer to be "free" of *obligations* to others. (responsibilities, duties)

8. To keep a friend, Americans are careful not to borrow or to *owe* too much money or too many favors. (be in debt; after borrowing money, one *owes* it until paying it back)

9. Jim's *refusal* to accept José's generosity made José question if they were really friends. (saying no)

10. Americans do not feel it is right to *rely* on others for too much. (depend on, take things from, count on) The value of *self-reliance* is very important to Americans. (being able to get along without having to take things from other people; independence in the sense of not having to ask other people for help)

11. I will feel that there is no *trust* between us. (the feeling that you can depend on another person)

Directions

In each numbered sentence below, fill in the blank with the best word from the vocabulary list above. Change tense and number (singular or plural) where necessary.

1. Even though Americans have a tradition of self-reliance, it does not seem to bother them to _____ on banks to help them pay for their houses and their cars.

2. The average American who owns a home, for example, must pay the bank a large _____ over a period of years.

3. When an American _____ money from a bank to pay for a house, it is called a mortgage.

4. The monthly mortgage payment that homeowners must make to the bank is often the largest financial _____ that the average American family has.

5. Banks _____ money to homeowners for their mortgages.

CASE STUDY

José and Jim worked together in a restaurant. They had become friendly because both of them were also studying. Jim was studying business, and José was taking English classes and planned to study engineering.

One day, as they were leaving work, Jim asked José, "José, I need a favor. I have to go over to school, and I'm out of money. Could you lend me a dollar so I can take the bus over there and then get home? I'll pay you back tomorrow."

"Sure, Jim. No problem. You don't have to pay me back," said José, as he handed Jim a dollar.

As soon as he got to work the next day, Jim went over to José and handed him a dollar, saying, "Thanks, José. I really appreciated this last night. It sure was too cold to walk."

"Forget it," said José, as he handed Jim back his dollar.

"Oh, no, I insist. I don't want to take advantage of a friend. What if I needed to borrow money again sometime? If I didn't pay you back now, I would feel wrong asking to borrow money again," said Jim, as he put the dollar into José's shirt pocket.

José answered, "But that's what friends are for. In Spanish, we have a saying, 'today for you, tomorrow for me.' If you pay me back, I will feel that I won't be able to ask you for money when I need it. I will feel like you are closing the door on me, that there is no trust between us. I thought we were friends. How can I take the money?" José handed back the dollar.

"But I won't feel right if you *don't* take it!" said Jim.

Questions

1. Why did Jim insist on returning the dollar to José?
2. Why did José not want to take it?
3. Do you think that their attitudes are cultural?
4. What cultural values are reflected in Jim's and José's attitudes?

BACKGROUND

One reason José did not want to accept Jim's dollar was that in his culture it is very important to be generous. Generosity, and respect for others' generosity, are two values that explain many Hispanic and Middle Eastern customs and attitudes. That is why Jim's refusal to accept José's generosity made José question their friendship. In cultures where generosity is such an important value, most people do not like to think of themselves as stingy or cheap, and these are terrible insults to a Hispanic or an Arab. In *Nonverbal Communication,* Carmen Judith Nine Curt writes that one reason Latins do not try to return small amounts of money is that one does not want to suggest that the other person is stingy. To a Latin, Jim's insistence on returning the dollar might mean that Jim thought José was stingy and had to have his dollar back.

Americans see it all differently. Jim felt that it would be rude if he did *not* try to return the dollar as soon as possible. To understand the American point of view, it is necessary to know how important the value of self-reliance is to Americans. Americans do not feel it is right to rely on others for too much. In American culture, owing too many favors means being dependent. Americans see this as a weakness. They do not like to think of themselves as "sponges" or "mooches," words used to describe people who take too much from other people. Americans cannot respect themselves if they feel too much "in debt" to other people, financially or otherwise. Instead, they prefer to be "free" of obligations to others. Americans feel strongly about paying their own way. To let someone else pay for them is "to take advantage," which is morally wrong. But if Jim and José were close friends, Jim would feel that he was not taking advantage of José. He would not need to pay back the dollar.

The case study is an example of two culturally different attitudes toward money. But it also shows something about two culturally different ideas about friendship. To José, giving Jim money when he needed it meant a way to build their friendship. In Latin cultures, instead of paying back the dollar, Jim would later do a favor for José, and José would then do Jim another favor, and so on. Friendship in Latin culture is based on the concept of interdependence and mutual obligation, much like the relations in Latin family life. Americans, on the other hand, often feel that too much dependence on another person, especially financial dependence, can hurt a friendship. To keep a friend, Americans are careful not to borrow or to owe too much money or too many favors.

PREINTERVIEW VOCABULARY EXERCISE

Study the sentences below. The words in *italics* are defined in parentheses.

appropriate — bargain — hippy — negotiate — privacy — signal — social mobility — social status — tip

1. Is it ever *appropriate* to give money to a government employee in order to get a job done well? (all right, correct in a certain situation)

2. In what situations is it not appropriate to try to *bargain?* (to offer less money than the price given)

3. The *hippies'* word for money was "bread." (a group of people who wore their hair very long and opposed many traditional American values during the 1960s)

4. In what situations would you try to *negotiate* the price of something? (change, argue)

5. The American value of *privacy* may explain why Americans do not like to be asked how much money their houses cost. (respect for keeping personal information secret)

6. When you are out with friends, what *signals* do you use to indicate who is paying? (words or gestures)

7. Perhaps because the United States is such a new country, there is more *social mobility* there than in some older cultures. (movement of people from one social class to another)

8. In your culture, does having a lot of money give people *social status?* (importance; high social class)

9. In the United States is it ever appropriate to *tip* a government employee in order to get a job done well? (give a sum of money)

Directions

In each numbered sentence below, fill in the blank with the best word from the vocabulary list above. Change tense as well as number (singular or plural) where necessary.

1. Because of _____ , the average American who buys a house lives in it for only 5 years.

2. In the American way of thinking, an expensive home proves that someone has a high _____ .

3. Because the cost of a home is so closely connected with a person's social status in the United States, it is almost never _____ to ask how much it cost.

4. An American thinks that to ask someone how much his house cost shows no respect for a person's _____ .

5. When buying a house in the United States, it is foolish not to try to _____ a better price.

Interviews and Analysis

• QUESTIONNAIRE 1 •
SOME ATTITUDES ABOUT MONEY

Answer the following questions yourself. Or interview a classmate from a different culture.

1. If you asked a friend (of the same sex) if he or she wanted to go out for lunch, and the friend agreed, who would pay when the bill came? Why? Is that the usual custom in your culture?

2. When you are out with friends, what signals do you use to indicate who is paying?

3. If you went out on a date to the movies, who would pay? Why? Is that the usual custom in your culture?

4. If you borrowed a dime from a friend to make a phone call, would you return the money the next time you saw your friend? Why or why not? Would your friend accept it? Why or why not?

5. If you needed $25 for an emergency, from whom would you try to borrow the money? What would happen if you did not pay it back?

6. In your culture, does having a lot of money give people social status? Explain.

7. Is it O.K. to ask a friend how much money he makes per month? If not, why not?

8. Would you ever ask a friend how much money his father makes? If not, why not?

9. How would you feel if a guest at your house asked you how much you had paid for your stereo?

10. Suppose you liked one particular teacher very much, and at the end of the semester you wanted to thank her in some way. Would you buy her a gift? How much is the least amount of money that you would spend? Why? How much is the most that you would spend? Why?

11. In what situations would you give someone a tip? How much would you tip?

12. In your culture, is it ever appropriate to tip a government employee in order to get a job done well or quickly? Explain.

13. According to the customs of your native culture, in what situations would you try to negotiate the price of something? In what situations is it not appropriate to try to bargain?

Name: _____ Culture: _____

• QUESTIONNAIRE 2•
SOME AMERICAN ATTITUDES ABOUT MONEY

Interview an American with the following questions, including a question of your own at the end. Write down any new vocabulary you hear or learn in the course of the interview.

1. If you asked a friend (of the same sex) if he or she wanted to go out for lunch, and the friend agreed, who would pay when the bill came? Why? Is that the usual custom in the United States?

2. When you are out with friends, what signals do you use to indicate who is paying?

3. If you went out on a date to the movies, who would pay? Why? Is that the usual custom in the United States?

4. If you borrowed a dime from a friend to make a phone call, would you return the money the next time you saw your friend? Why or why not? Would your friend accept it? Why or why not?

5. If you needed $25 for an emergency, from whom would you try to borrow the money? What would happen if you did not pay it back?

6. In the United States, do you think that having a lot of money gives people social status? Explain.

7. Is it O.K. to ask a friend how much money he makes per month? If not, why not?

8. Would you ever ask a friend how much money his father makes? If not, why not?

9. How would you feel if a guest at your house asked you how much you had paid for your stereo?

10. Suppose you liked one particular teacher very much and at the end of the semester you wanted to thank her in some way. Would you

buy her a gift? How much is the least amount of money that you would spend? Why? How much is the most that you would spend? Why?

11. In what situations would you give someone a tip? How much would you tip?

12. In the United States is it ever appropriate to tip a government employee in order to get a job done well or quickly? Explain.

13. In what sorts of situations do Americans try to negotiate the price of something? In what situations is it not appropriate to try to bargain?

14. (Your own question)

Person interviewed: _____ Age: _____

Sex: _____ Ethnic background: _____

Father's work: _____

New vocabulary

INDIVIDUAL ANALYSIS

Compare the answers given by the American you interviewed with the answers that someone from your culture would give to the same questions. Then answer these questions.

1. Which questions would someone from your culture answer the same as the American you interviewed?

2. Which questions would someone from your culture answer differently from the American you interviewed?

3. Choose two questions that would be answered differently and give the explanations for each answer. That is, take the American answer and explain it from the American point of view, and then give the most typical answer from your culture and explain it from that point of view.

GROUP ANALYSIS

In class, share the responses from all the interviews with Americans. Then answer these questions.

1. The way that people answer the questions on the questionnaire shows their cultural values. What American values help explain the most common answers to the questions? Some of the values you might consider are sexual equality, independence, thrift, social mobility, generosity, chivalry, and privacy.

2. Compare the answers to the questions made up by individuals in the class. What values do these represent?

3. To which questions did some Americans have very different answers than others? Can you explain any of these differences by the sex, age, social class, or background of the Americans interviewed?

Additional Activities

LETTER OF ADVICE

Imagine that your cousin is moving to the United States. Write him or her a letter of advice on adjusting to American customs and attitudes regarding money. Advise your cousin about what to do as well as what not to do.

DICTIONARY OF SLANG

The hippies' word for money was "bread," while the more traditional slang term is "dough" (which is unbaked bread). Can you find out any other slang words used in connection with money?

SYMBOLISM ON UNITED STATES CURRENCY

Research the meanings of the symbols on the United States coins and bills. For example, what people appear on the money and what was their role in U.S. history? What animal or animals are portrayed, and why? Whose signature appears and why? What is the motto?

In Conclusion

What cultural misunderstandings could occur between someone from your culture and an American, based on different customs or attitudes related to money? Give an example. How would the misunderstandings add to the negative stereotypes that each group might already have about the other?

Chapter 9

Eating in the
United States

What are some of your observations about eating in the United States? Write three sentences about your impressions of what, when, and how Americans eat.

Preparation

PREREADING VOCABULARY EXERCISE

Study the sentences below. The words in *italics* are defined in parentheses.

> barbecue — croissant — dish — fresh — health food — junk food —
> nut — pot luck — processed — sour cream — TV dinner

1. "I'll *barbecue* hot dogs and hamburgers." (cook on an open fire)

2. The French might not recognize the *croissants* served at McDonald's. (a French crescent-shaped roll)

3. Jeanette was preparing her *dish.* (food made in a certain way)

4. The time saved by opening a can of peas was more important to busy housewives than was the better taste of *fresh* peas. (food recently picked)

5. *Health foods* may be popular today because many Americans are tired of processed foods like Rick's California dip. (foods made from fresh ingredients, often containing no meat, sugar, or preservatives)

114

6. Rick just can't live without *junk food.* (food such as candy bars that makes one gain weight without giving the body what it needs)

7. "Jeanette's a health food *nut!*" (someone who feels so strongly about something that he or she seems a little crazy)

8. The rest of the party is *pot luck.* (each guest brings some food)

9. It is made only from natural, not *processed,* foods. (foods that are treated in some way at the factory)

10. Rick walked into the kitchen and started mixing a package of dried mushroom soup with some *sour cream.* (a milk product made from heavy cream)

11. Many prefer frozen pizzas, potato chips, and *TV dinners.* (frozen dinners sold at American supermarkets)

Directions

In each numbered sentence below, fill in the blank with the best word from the vocabulary list above. Change tense and number (singular or plural) where necessary.

1. Many Americans today are _____ about Chinese food.

2. For one thing, every Chinese _____ is made from natural foods.

3. Very few Chinese foods are _____ in factories.

4. Almost all the vegetables used are _____ .

5. But while more Americans enjoy Chinese food all the time, many Chinese-American children are learning to like American_____ like potato chips.

CASE STUDY

At the end of her first semester in an American college, Elsa, a student from Greece, was surprised to hear her chemistry professor invite the whole class to a party at his house.

"I hope you all will be able to come," he announced. "I'll barbecue hot dogs and hamburgers, but the rest is pot luck. I hope we have some good cooks here!"

Elsa was happy to have the chance to try some real American home cooking after eating in the college cafeteria all semester. She wanted to see what real American food was like.

The morning of the party, Elsa prepared a traditional Greek spinach pie, *spanakopitta*. An American classmate, Jeanette, had invited her to cook it in her kitchen. While Elsa cooked, Jeanette was preparing her dish for the party, a salad called *tabbouleh*.

"But I used to eat a salad just like that in Greece!" laughed Elsa, when she saw Jeanette washing the tomatoes. "Is that a typical American dish?"

"No, it's Middle Eastern. But my grandmother is from Lebanon, and it's always been my favorite salad. And now it's quite popular. I even saw it on the menu at school," said Jeanette.

Jeanette's boyfriend, Rick, walked into the kitchen and started mixing a package of dried mushroom soup with some sour cream. "This is called California dip," he explained to Elsa. "I'm going to buy potato chips to eat it with. I probably should go buy some carrots and celery, too, to serve with the dip. But it's so much work to wash them and cut them up."

"I hope you don't get the wrong idea of American food, Elsa. Rick just can't live without junk food!" said Jeanette.

"Yeah, and Jeanette's a health food nut!" answered Rick.

Questions

1. Why was Elsa surprised that her professor invited the class to a party?
2. Do you think it is a formal or an informal party? Do you think that it would be O.K. to wear blue jeans to such a party?
3. When Jeanette said, "I hope you don't get the wrong idea of American food," what did she mean?
4. Do Jeanette and Rick enjoy the same foods?
5. Do you think that Jeanette and Rick helped Elsa get a better idea of what Americans eat?

BACKGROUND

Jeanette's tabbouleh salad and Rick's California dip are examples of two kinds of food popular in the United States today. International, or "ethnic," dishes, like Jeanette's Lebanese salad, have become quite popular with Americans in recent years. Of course, Americans cook them their own way. The French might not recognize the croissants served at McDonald's, for example. And indeed, throughout United States history, certain foreign foods have become all-American favorites: pizza comes from Italy, and the first fried chicken in America was probably cooked by Africans.

Jeanette's grandmother's dish, tabbouleh, is not as popular or well known as pizza. But some Americans like it because they consider it a health food: it is made from only natural, not processed, foods. More and more Americans are interested in foods that have spent more time at the farm than at the factory.

Health foods may be popular today because many Americans became tired of processed foods like Rick's California dip. Canned, frozen, and processed foods became very popular in the United States in the 1950s. At that time, the American food industry tried to convince American cooks that these foods were more timesaving, modern, and safe. And those values were more important to most Americans than the taste of the food. The time saved by opening a can of peas was more important to busy housewives than the better taste of fresh peas, which take more work in the kitchen. And the economy of the United States changed so that it actually became cheaper to buy canned or frozen peas than fresh ones.

What do Americans eat today? Many, like Rick, who grew up eating food out of a can, prefer frozen pizzas, potato chips, and TV dinners. Others prefer "plain old American food," which usually means something like simply cooked meat with potatoes and vegetables cooked separately. At the same time, some Americans, like Jeanette, have become interested in other kinds of foods, such as health foods and international foods.

PREINTERVIEW VOCABULARY EXERCISE

Study the sentences below. The words in *italics* are defined in parentheses.

avoid — balanced meal — belch — diet — helping — home remedy — lap — lick — recipe — slurp — snack — taboo — treat

1. What foods do you try to *avoid?* (stay away from)
2. What is a *balanced meal?* (a meal having all the right kinds of foods for good health)
3. What would you think if your guest *belched* after the meal? (made a noise when air came up from the stomach)
4. Do you think most Americans eat a healthy *diet?* (the foods that people eat every day; sometimes it means the foods that people eat to lose weight)
5. What do you think if your guest asks for a second *helping?* (a serving of more food)
6. What foods or *home remedies* are said to be good for a cold? (homemade medicines; traditional cures such as special teas)
7. Do you keep one hand in your *lap* while eating? (the upper part of your legs when you are seated)
8. She *licked* the gravy from her fingers. (touch with the tongue outside the mouth)
9. Would you ever ask for the *recipe?* (directions for making a dish)
10. Is it all right to make *slurping* sounds while eating? (to make noises when eating soup or other foods with liquids)
11. What is your favorite *snack?* (foods eaten between meals)
12. What foods or meats are *taboo* to most Americans? (never eaten, because people think they are disgusting)

13. When you were a child, what foods did your mother prepare as a special *treat?* (something special, not eaten every day)

Directions

In each numbered sentence below, fill in the blank with the best word from the vocabulary list above. Change tense and number (singular and plural) where necessary.

1. "Boy, do I love ice cream!" cried Karen as she _____ her cone with her tongue.

2. "Me too!" agreed Jenny as she _____ her ice cream soda.

3. "This is a real_____ for me. I try not to eat it too often so I won't get fat," said Karen.

4. "Well, I try to only have it for dessert, not as a _____ at night," added Jenny.

5. "Just think, Jenny. If we didn't try to _____ ice cream, it probably wouldn't taste so good when we finally had it!"

Interviews and Analysis

GENERAL INSTRUCTIONS FOR INTERVIEWS

On the pages that follow there are four questionnaires: Questionnaire 1: American Meals and Mealtimes; Questionnaire 2: What Do Americans Eat? Questionnaire 3: American Table Manners; Questionnaire 4: American Views on Food and Health. Choose the topic that interests you most, and interview an American, using one of the questionnaires. Make up one question of your own and write down any new vocabulary. In class, get together with other students who interviewed with the same questionnaire. Together, analyze the answers given by the Americans and plan a report.

• QUESTIONNAIRE 1 •
AMERICAN MEALS AND MEALTIMES

1. In your household, at what time is breakfast? Lunch? Dinner?

2. Which is the main meal? Is it always?

3. At which meals do all the people in your household sit down to eat together? How long do you usually spend at the table?

4. When your whole household eats together, who generally does the cooking? Who serves? Who washes the dishes?

5. Does everyone sit in certain chairs? Explain. Where would a guest sit?

6. How often do you eat between meals? What is your favorite snack?

7. How often do you eat out? Where do you usually go?

8. When you were growing up, what meals did your family eat together? Who talked? What did they talk about?

9. How were family meals served? Who did the cooking? Who washed the dishes?

10. Does your family observe any special customs at mealtimes, such as saying grace?

11. (Your own question)

Person interviewed: _____ Sex: _____

Age: _____ Ethnic background: _____

New vocabulary

• QUESTIONNAIRE 2 •
WHAT DO AMERICANS EAT?

1. What is your favorite breakfast? Your favorite lunch? Your favorite dinner? Your favorite dessert? Your favorite snack? How often do you get to eat your favorite foods?

2. What foods do you try to avoid? Why?

3. When you were a child, what foods did your mother prepare as a special treat? What were your grandmother's special dishes? What is your family's ethnic background?

4. What are some of the traditional foods in your family that are prepared for the different holidays?

5. Do you know if this part of the country is famous for any dish in particular?

6. What are some examples (such as Southern fried chicken) of other regional cooking in the United States?

7. What local restaurant serves good American food?

8. Do you think that Americans today eat differently than they did in the past? If so, how?

9. What foods or meats are taboo to most Americans?

10. Are you a vegetarian? Do you know any? Do you know why they are vegetarians?

11. (Your own question)

Person interviewed: _____ Sex: _____

Age: _____ Ethnic background: _____

New vocabulary

• QUESTIONNAIRE 3 •
AMERICAN TABLE MANNERS

Special note

Be sure to ask the American you are interviewing to explain any custom that you don't understand.

1. Suppose that you have invited guests for dinner. Would you consider it good manners, bad manners, or unimportant if one of your guests did the following:

    a. waited for you to tell him or her where to sit

    b. served him or herself instead of waiting to be served

    c. started eating before everyone was served

    d. talked with food in his or her mouth

    e. picked up a chicken wing with his or her fingers

    f. dipped his or her bread into the gravy

    g. made slurping sounds while eating

    h. kept one hand in his or her lap while eating

    i. cut meat with the fork in the left hand and then changed the fork to the right before bringing the food to his or her mouth

    j. picked up bread with his or her left hand

    k. commented on how good the food was

    l. asked for the recipe

    m. finished everything on the plate

    n. said no thanks to more food

    o. put his or her elbows on the table

    p. described a bloody accident scene during dinner

    q. asked for a second helping

    r. licked some gravy off his or her fingers

    s. left the table to go to the bathroom in the middle of the meal

    t. ate very quickly

    u. ate very slowly

    v. belched after the meal

2. What are some examples of bad manners besides some of the ones just mentioned?

3. What are some other examples of good manners?

4. As a child, what table manners did your parents make sure you learned?

5. (Your own question)

Person interviewed: _____ Sex: _____

Age: _____ Ethnic background: _____

New vocabulary

• QUESTIONNAIRE 4 •
AMERICAN VIEWS ON FOOD AND HEALTH

1. What foods, drinks, vitamins, or home remedies are said to be good for:

   a. a cold

   b. a fever

c. a headache

d. a sore throat

e. an upset stomach

f. tiredness

g. losing weight

h. gaining weight

i. for athletes in training

j. for pregnant women

2. What are health foods? Give some examples. Do you yourself eat any health foods?

3. Do you try to avoid certain foods for health reasons? Which ones? Why?

4. Do you think most Americans eat a healthy diet? Why or why not?

5. Do most Americans worry more about being too fat or about being too thin? Why?

6. Do you watch your weight? How?

7. What is a balanced meal? Give an example.

8. What foods and drinks do Americans believe should not be given to babies and very young children?

9. (Your own question)

Person interviewed: _____ Sex: _____

Age: _____ Ethnic background: _____

New vocabulary

GROUP ANALYSIS

Compare the answers given to the questionnaire by Americans interviewed by members of your group. Prepare a report from your group's discussion of the following questions:

1. What were the most common, or typical answers to each question?

2. a. In what ways are these answers different from the customs of students in the group?

   b. In what ways are these answers similar to some students' customs?

3. If some Americans answered questions differently from the way others did, can you tell if these differences could be explained by the ethnic backgrounds of the people interviewed?

4. Does the United States history as a nation of immigrants from all over the world show in what Americans eat? If so, how?

Additional Activities

ADDITIONAL INTERVIEWS

Make up your own questionnaire on another topic related to eating. One possible topic is American cooking (ask about the most important condiments, cooking methods, utensils; food shopping; gourmet cooking). Another topic is restaurants: recommendations of the best local restaurants; different varieties of restaurants; etiquette in restaurants such as tipping and dress codes. Then interview one or more Americans using your questionnaire.

RESTAURANT VISIT

With the members of your group, visit a restaurant recommended by Americans for serving good American food. Ask the waiter to serve you the most typically American choices on the menu, and share examples of each among the group.

CLASS COOKBOOK

Put together a class cookbook of popular or traditional American dishes. Obtain the recipes from cookbooks or from good American cooks. Or make up an international cookbook, choosing just one type of food, such as rice dishes. Ask your classmates and some Americans for recipes.

ROLE PLAY

Role-play the following situations:

1. American table manners
2. Good table manners in other cultures
3. An American eating a meal as the guest of someone from another culture whose table manners are quite different

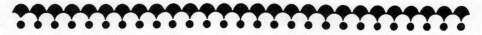

In Conclusion

Look back to the three impressions of what, when, and how Americans eat that you wrote down on page 114. Do you still agree with these comments after studying more about American eating, or would you change them in any way? If so, how would you change them? Did you learn anything that surprised you about how and what Americans eat? If so, what?

Chapter 10

Immigrant Experiences: Past and Present

Ellis Island, N.Y.: A turn-of-the-century Italian immigrant family getting off the boat

Los Angeles International Airport: A recent Chinese refugee family from Vietnam arriving in the U.S. by plane

Both these families arrived hoping to build a new and better life in the United States. What do you think might be the same for both families? What might be different for them?

Preparation

PREREADING VOCABULARY EXERCISE

Study the sentences below. The words in *italics* are defined in parentheses.

> *adjust — birthrate — conflict — descendant/descended from — discriminate/discrimination/discriminatory — economy — illegally — immigrant/immigrate/immigration — manual labor — migrant — permission — previous/previously — restrict — undocumented —*

1. All have had to *adjust* to a new life in a new culture. (get used to, fit into)
2. The higher *birthrate* of Americans of color is changing the racial mix of the United States. (percent of new babies born in the population)
3. There was a *conflict* between an immigrant father and his American-born teenaged son. (a situation where two people cannot agree, a disagreement)

4. Most Black Americans are the *descendants* of African slaves. (children, grandchildren, great-grandchildren, etc.; people born from others) A large number of Hispanic-Americans are *descended from* families that lived in the region that is now Texas. (come from; are directly related by birth)

5. Many have had to face *discrimination* against their racial, ethnic, or religious group. (different or unfair treatment because of race or sex) *Discriminatory* signs like that are against the law. (unfair, unequal, unjust) Some employers still *discriminate* against immigrants. (treat badly because of race or sex)

6. The American *economy* is not growing as fast as it once was. (system of businesses, agriculture, and government that produces jobs)

7. Many Central Americans, Haitians, and Mexicans who had to leave their countries because of poverty or the political situation must live in the United States *illegally*. (against the law, without the permission of the United States government)

8. Most *immigrants* have looked for help and support from other *immigrants*. (people who move from one country or region to another with the purpose of staying, or settling there) In almost all families that have ever *immigrated* to the United States there have been conflicts. (moved with the idea of staying in another place) There have been changes in the *immigration* laws. (the act of coming to a new country to settle there)

9. Eighty years ago an immigrant with a fifth-grade education could support a large family by doing *manual labor*. (work with one's hands, such as construction work)

10. Puerto Ricans who leave the island for New York or Boston are *migrants*, not immigrants. (people who move within one country or region)

11. Did you ask your father's *permission* to go? (consent; when someone allows someone else to do something)

12. The majority of *previous* immigrants to the United States came from Europe. (from before; former; last) Do you know what kind of work they had done *previously*? (before)

13. The U.S. Department of Immigration made a decision to *restrict* the number of immigrants. (to keep small, to limit)

14. The experience of these *undocumented* immigrants is naturally quite different from the experience of immigrants who were welcomed by the United States. (without legal papers; illegal)

Directions

In each numbered sentence below, fill in the blank with the best word in parentheses. Change singular to plural if necessary. Read the example.

Example: **(immigrant, immigration, immigrate)** There are many different reasons why people _immigrate_ to the United States every year.

1. **(immigrant, immigration, migrate)** One reason is religious freedom, and some of the first _____ to the New World were the Puritans, who had to leave England because of their religion.

2. **(immigrant, immigration, migrate)** Religious freedom also explains the _____ to the United States by Jews who were discriminated against in Europe.

3. **(immigrant, immigration, migrate)** Puerto Ricans, on the other hand, _____ to the mainland mainly because of economic reasons.

4. **(descendants, descend)** Most Irish left their native land for the same reason as Puerto Ricans, and many Irish-Americans are _____ of people who came to the United States so that they could get enough to eat.

5. **(descendants, descend)** Many Italian-Americans, too, _____ from immigrants who hoped to find better economic opportunities.

CASE STUDY

One Friday, Milagros Ruiz, a Cuban-American teenager, came home after school. Her mother met her at the door and gave her daughter a big kiss. Milagros looked uncomfortable.

"Oh, Mom, I'm too old for that. My American friends can't believe I still kiss my mother as if I were six years old," said Milagros in English.

Her mother looked hurt. In Spanish, she said, "Come in the kitchen and have something to eat. I've just made roast pork."

"Thanks, Mom, but I'm on a diet. I don't have time, anyway. I have to go shopping to buy something to wear for the dance at school tonight. I just came home to get my money," answered Milagros in English.

"What dance? Did you ask your father's permission to go? I don't think he's free tonight, and you know he won't let you go by yourself."

"I can't believe this! We're not living in the year 1800. Times have changed, Mom. Here in the United States, anyway. Nobody's father goes to the dance with them. Don't you trust me?"

"It's not that, but you know how your father is. Back in Cuba, a good girl from a good family would never go out alone. Let me see if maybe your brother could go with you instead, O.K.?"

"Thanks, Mom. I'm going shopping now."

"Don't buy anything too short, dear. You know your father won't let you wear it," warned Mrs. Ruiz.

"But it's the style! All the kids will laugh at me if I wear something too long. It just isn't fair!"

Questions

1. Why do you think Milagros spoke in English while her mother spoke in Spanish?
2. Why was her mother hurt?
3. What were the conflicts in Milagros' life?
4. Can you guess about the conflicts for her parents?
5. Is there a way for the Ruiz family to solve their conflicts?

BACKGROUND

In almost all families that have ever immigrated to the United States there have been conflicts like those in the Ruiz family. In immigrant families, the children are often pulled in two directions at once. They are pulled from one side by their family's culture and from the other side by the American culture they learn in school. And all immigrant parents and children have to decide how to resolve these intercultural conflicts so that they are not pulled apart.

There are other similarities in the experiences of immigrants past and present. All have come with hopes for a better life, especially for their children. All have had to adjust to a new life in a new culture. Most have looked for help and support from other immigrants. Many have had to face discrimination against their racial, ethnic, or religious group. For example, when many Irish began to immigrate to the United States, some American factories hung signs that said "No Irish Need Apply." Today, discriminatory signs like that are against the law, but some employers still discriminate against immigrants.

Yet there are differences, too, in the immigration experience, past and present. One difference is economic opportunity. The American economy is not growing as fast as it once was, and so there are not as many good jobs open to people who do not know English. Eighty years ago an immigrant with a fifth-grade education could support a large family doing manual labor; this is much more difficult today. A second difference is the U.S. Department of Immigration's decision to restrict the number of immigrants. Therefore, many Central Americans, Haitians, and Mexicans who had to leave their countries because of poverty or the political situation must live in the United States illegally, without the necessary papers. The experience of these undocumented immigrants is naturally quite different from the experience of European immigrants a hundred years ago who were welcomed by the United States with open arms.

Another difference is skin color. Because the majority of previous American immigrants came from Europe, their children did not look different from most Americans and were accepted as Americans. Many of today's immigrants must face the problem of racial discrimination. The majority of today's immigrants, Asians and Hispanics, are people of color. These new immigrants, and the higher birthrate of Americans of color, are changing the racial mix of the United States. According to the United States Census Bureau, in less than a hundred years, the majority of the U.S. population will be people of color.

Of course, not all American families immigrated here at one time. Indians, who prefer the name Native Americans, had their own culture in the New World when Christopher Columbus "discovered" America. Long, long ago Native Americans may have come from Asia. Most Black Americans are the descendants of African slaves who were brought here by force—they did not choose to immigrate. Other Black Americans, though, have immigrated to the United States: from the West Indies, Cape Verde, Haiti, and Africa. A large number of Hispanic Americans are descended from families that lived in the region that is now Texas, New Mexico, Arizona, and California, before that land was sold to the United States by Mexico, in 1848. In that year, thousands of Mexicans became Americans overnight, without actually immigrating. Finally, the more than 1 million Puerto Ricans who have moved from the island are all citizens of the United States, as are all Puerto Ricans born in Puerto Rico. Thus Puerto Ricans who leave the island are migrants, not immigrants, although in some ways their experiences may be similar to experiences of immigrants to the United States.

PREINTERVIEW VOCABULARY EXERCISE

Study the sentences below. The words in *italics* are defined in parentheses.

> *conditions — generation — miss — originally — permanent resident —*
> *pass on — refugee — roots — struggle*

1. The United States has let in some immigrants because of special *conditions*. (situation; circumstances; things happening)
2. What was the native language of the first *generation* of your family who

came to the United States? (a group of people of about the same age, that is, not including parents or children)

3. What do you *miss* most about life in your native country? (feel sad about the absence of something or someone)

4. Where did your family come from *originally?* (before coming here, in this case, before coming to the United States)

5. Was it difficult to get permission to become a *permanent resident?* (a person with the legal right to stay in the United States for a long time)

6. What cultural traditions would you like to *pass on* to your children? (to give)

7. Many European *refugees* from World War II were allowed to enter the United States. (people who must leave their countries for their own safety)

8. A grandmother from the old country tells her American grandchildren that they should not forget their *roots.* (who and where one comes from)

9. What would you say was lost as your family *struggled* to become Americans? (worked hard)

Directions

In each numbered sentence below, fill in the blank with the best word from the vocabulary list above. Change tense and number (singular and plural) where necessary.

1. Since 1970, the largest number of immigrants to the United States have

   been _____ from Vietnam.

2. Many of the Vietnamese have _____ very hard first to leave

   Vietnam and then again to get into the United States.

3. Once they finally get permission to enter, most Vietnamese can become

   _____ of the United States.

4. Although they are glad about the political freedom in the United States,

   many Vietnamese _____ the family and culture they had to leave

   behind.

5. Because they respect their culture, many Vietnamese try to _____

   traditional values and customs to their children.

Interviews and Analysis

• QUESTIONNAIRE 1 •
EXPERIENCES OF AN IMMIGRANT TODAY

If you are an immigrant to the United States yourself, answer the questionnaire from your own experiences. If you do not plan on staying in the United States, interview an immigrant (or a Puerto Rican living in the United States who was born on the island).

Part I: The Move

1. Where were you born?

2. When did you come to the United States?

3. How did you get to the United States? Was it difficult to get permission to become a permanent resident?

4. Who did you come with?

5. Where did you live when you first arrived? Why did you decide to live there?

6. What would you tell someone from your home town who wanted to move to the United States?

7. Why did you decide to come to the United States?

Part II: The Adjustment

8. Did you find what you were looking for in the United States? Please explain.

9. What has been most difficult for you to get used to here? What do you miss most about life in your native country?

10. Do you have a lot of contact with others who came from your native country? In what ways do you help each other out?

11. Have any American agencies or government programs helped you since you arrived?

12. What jobs have you been able to find here? What kind of work did you do before?

13. Do you still have contact with family in your native country?

14. What cultural traditions would you like to pass on to your children?

15. How have you changed since coming to the United States?

16. What do you like best about life in the United States?

Name: _____

•QUESTIONNAIRE 2•
EXPERIENCES OF PAST IMMIGRANTS

Interview an American who was born in the United States, if possible, an older person. Make up one question yourself, and list the new vocabulary in the space at the end.

Part I: The Move

1. Where did your family come from originally?

2. Do you know in what year (or years) they came to the United States?

3. Do you know how they came? Do you know if it was difficult for them to get permission to enter the United States?

4. Do you know who in your family came first and who else they came with?

5. Do you know where they lived when they first arrived? Why did they live there?

6. Did you ever hear any family stories about life in the old country? If so, what was it like?

7. Do you know the reason or reasons that your family left their native land?

Part II: The Adjustment

8. Do you think that the first generation of family members who immigrated to the United States found what they were looking for?

9. Do you know of any difficulties that they had as immigrants?

10. Did they have much contact with other immigrants from their native country? Do you know if they helped each other out?

11. Did any American agencies or government programs help them out?

12. Do you know what jobs they held when they first got to the United States? Do you know what kind of work they had done previously?

13. Does anyone in your family still have contact with family members back in the old country?

14. Do you feel _____? (fill in the ethnic background of the person you are interviewing, such as Chinese or French) If so, how? What cultural traditions have been passed down to you, if any?

15. What would you say was lost as your family struggled to become Americans?

16. What was the native language of the first generation of your family who came to the United States? Do you, or does anyone in your

family, still speak it? Do you know if the first generation of your family to come to the United States learned English well?

17. (Your own question)

Person interviewed: _____

New vocabulary

INDIVIDUAL ANALYSIS

Compare the answers to each question on Questionnaires 1 and 2, and answer:

1. Are any of the experiences of the two families who left their native lands to come to the United States similar? List some similarities.

2. How are their experiences different?

3. Do you think that immigrants today should try harder to keep their culture and language than the immigrants of the past did? Why or why not?

4. What are the difficulties that immigrants might face if they want to keep their language and culture?

GROUP ANALYSIS

In class, share the answers given to both questionnaires, including the questions that students made up themselves. Because there is so much information to discuss, it may be easier to divide the class into smaller groups to share the answers to the questionnaires and to discuss the following questions:

1. What are the main reasons people came to the United States in the past?

2. What are the main reasons that people have been coming recently?

3. What were some of the difficulties that immigrants faced in the past?

4. What are some of the difficulties that immigrants face today?

5. What are some of the cultural traditions that immigrants of previous generations passed on to their descendants?

6. Will the descendants of today's immigrants keep their culture and/or their language more than the descendants of past immigrants did? Why or why not?

Additional Activities

ROLE PLAY

Based on your information from the interviews, role-play any of the following situations two ways, according to the experiences of two of the ethnic groups that answered the questionnaires.

1. A conflict between an immigrant father and his American-born teenaged son

2. A family trying to decide whether or not to move to the United States

3. An immigrant grandmother telling her American grandchildren that they should not forget their roots

4. An immigrant family going back to their native country for a visit after living in the United States for 15 years

RESEARCH PROJECT

Research the present immigration law. (The local Immigration and Naturalization Service should be able to help you.) Then look up information in an encyclopedia about the previous U.S. laws, such as those of 1924 and 1965. Do you feel that the present law is fair or not? How would you change it? Explain.

ADDITIONAL INTERVIEW

Do any schools in your area offer bilingual education programs? (In American bilingual programs, students learn in two languages: their own language and English.) Interview a bilingual teacher, a bilingual student, or the parent of a child in a bilingual program. Find out how the bilingual program works, its history, its advantages and its disadvantages.

ESSAY

At different times in the past 50 years, the United States has let in some immigrants because of special conditions. For example, many European refugees from World War II were allowed to enter the United States, as were Cubans who did not like the government of Fidel Castro, as well as Vietnamese, Cambodian, and Laotian refugees from the war in Indochina. Is there another group today that, in your opinion, should also be allowed to enter the United States because of special conditions? Explain the reasons in an essay.

In Conclusion

What were your personal feelings about the family experiences of the American you interviewed? What lessons, if any, do you think today's immigrants can learn from the experiences of previous generations of immigrants?

Chapter 11

Youth Culture

American youth culture 1969: hippy

American youth culture 1984: punk

In what ways—besides the way they wear their hair—do young people (ages 13 to 25) show the adult world that they belong to a "youth culture"?

Preparation

PREREADING VOCABULARY EXERCISE

Study the sentences below. The words in *italics* are defined in parentheses.

hassle — industry —lousy — product — punk — separate —traditional — upset

1. The only reason he was *hassling* me was my short hair! (bothering—a slang word)
2. Youth culture is also a large *industry* in the United States. (business)
3. A *lousy* thing happened today. (bad; *lousy* is a slang word)
4. Many American *products* are made especially for youth. (things to buy)
5. Mrs. Donovan never said anything about her son's *punk* haircut. (a style of music, dress, and very short hair that became popular in 1983)
6. To become independent, teenagers must *separate* themselves from their parents. (to grow apart, to become independent) American young people must show adults that they are *separate* from them. (independent)
7. Many American young people began wearing *traditional* American work pants worn by cowboys and farmers. (from the old culture, not modern)
8. Jack came home one day very *upset*. (unhappy)

Directions

In each numbered sentence below, fill in the blank with the best word from the above vocabulary list. Change tense and number (singular and plural) where necessary.

1. While an older person would say, "Don't bother me," a younger person might use the expression, "Don't _____ me."

2. Someone talking with friends might use the phrase "a _____ time" instead of "a bad time."

3. While the word "hassle" is new slang, the word "lousy" is a _____ American slang term.

4. "Lousy" is accepted in oral speech, but when used in writing it will make an English teacher very _____ .

5. It is often wise to use a _____ vocabulary for oral and written English.

CASE STUDY

Jack Donovan, an American teenager, came home one day very upset.

"Hi, dear, did you and your friends have a nice afternoon?" asked his mother.

"It was O.K.," answered Jack as he passed his mother at the front door. She heard him close the door to his room and turn on his favorite music.

Mrs. Donovan was not surprised that her son did not give her a nicer greeting. He did not really talk much to his parents anymore. His mother knew it was because of his age. That is why she did not try to stop Jack from spending so much time in his room by himself listening to loud music. She knew that bad moods are a part of growing up. And she understood that teenagers need time for themselves. Mrs. Donovan also never said anything about her son's punk haircut or about the torn old clothes he wore. She believed in letting him have his freedom.

But today she was worried. She thought that maybe there was really something wrong. She hoped that Jack was not taking drugs.

When Jack's father, Mr. Donovan, came home, his wife asked him to go in and talk to Jack.

Mr. Donovan knocked on Jack's door three times, but the music was playing so loudly that Jack couldn't hear the door. So Mr. Donovan just walked in.

"Hi, Jack. Could you turn that down a minute?"

"WHAT? I CAN'T HEAR YOU!"

Jack's father turned down the music. "How're you doing, Jack?"

"O.K., Dad. But a lousy thing happened today. I was standing in front of my friend Billy's apartment house waiting for him to come down. And a policeman started giving me a hard time for no reason at all. He told me to move. The only reason he was hassling me was because of my short hair!"

Mr. Donovan started laughing and laughing.

"What's so funny, Dad? How would you like people to treat you badly just because of your hair?"

"Well, that's what's so funny. They did. Back in 1968 and 1969, when I was a student, the police used to give *us* a hard time because our hair was too *long*. They thought we were *communists* if our hair was any longer than yours is now."

Jack smiled. "Boy, things have changed, haven't they?"

His father smiled back. "I'm not so sure."

Questions

1. Do you think Jack's mother cared about her son?
2. Why did she let him wear old clothes and spend so much time in his room by himself?
3. Why was Jack upset?
4. Why did Jack's father laugh?
5. What did his father mean when he said he wasn't sure things had changed?
6. Do most people in your culture agree with Mrs. Donovan's beliefs about youth?

BACKGROUND

Of course, not all American parents act like the Donovans. Many argue over their teenage sons' and daughters' choice of clothes, music, hours, friends, and habits. But almost all American parents do have one thing in common. They expect the teenage years to be a difficult time for the family.

Why is there so much conflict between American young people and their parents, between youth culture and the dominant American culture? One explanation is the importance of independence and individualism in American culture. In the United States, growing up means becoming independent, above all. To become independent, teenagers must separate themselves from their parents. That is why most American teenagers respect their friends' opinions more than the opinions of their parents. American youth culture—values, music, dances, clothing, even langauge—is American young people's way of showing adults that they are separate from them, that they are independent, because they are different. Jack's haircut was his way of showing that he was part of his friends' world now, not his parents'.

Youth culture is also a large industry in the United States. The record companies and the clothing industry alone make millions of dollars from American youth culture. For example, many American young people wear traditional American work pants that were worn by cowboys and farmers: blue jeans. They have become a very popular style among all Americans and around the world.

Like blue jeans, many other styles that began with American youth have spread around the world. One reason is that American businesses spend so much money on advertising. Another is that many American products are made especially for youth. American women's clothing, for example, has two kinds of sizes: "misses" sizes 4, 6, 8, 10, 12, 14, and 16 are for women, and "junior" sizes 3, 5, 7, 9, 11, 13, and 15, for teenaged girls and younger women. In many other countries, of course, teenaged girls just buy the same clothing as older women.

Another reason why some American youth culture styles are so popular in other parts of the world is the changes in traditional societies. As more people move to cities from farms, the family becomes less important economically. Therefore, children become less dependent on their families. Thus, many young people around the world, as in the United States, have become more interested in the international youth culture than in the traditional culture of their societies.

PREINTERVIEW VOCABULARY EXERCISE

Directions

Study the sentences below. The words in *italics* are defined in parentheses.

aspect — disagree — dress — last — rebel — style — wicked —

1. What *aspects* of American youth culture are popular among young people in your culture? (parts, such as the music or the dance)
2. If parents and teenagers *disagree*, what might they *disagree* about? (not agree; have different opinions about something)
3. Do young people *dress* differently from older people? (choose clothes to wear; wear clothes)

4. Do you think that these differences will *last*? (continue)

5. Do you or did you *rebel* as a teenager? (go against what people expect; act differently from the way most people do)

6. What are some of the most popular *styles* of dress, dance, music, and speech among American young people today? (popular way of doing something; fashion)

7. In some parts of the country, "a *wicked* good time" is used to mean "a very good time." (very evil)

Directions

Fill in the blanks in the following sentences with the best words from the vocabulary list above. Change tense and number (singular and plural) where necessary.

1. In America, it seems as if each generation must _____ against the generation that came before.

2. One can see examples of this kind of rebellion in the music that is popular among the youth, and in their _____ of dancing.

3. The way young people _____ is often very different from the clothes that the older generation might wear.

4. Sometimes the clothing fashions among young people do not_____ for more than a year; by the next year they are out of style.

5. But even if the clothes can only be worn for a few months, they are worth the price to American teenagers, who need something to _____ about with their parents.

Interviews and Analysis

• QUESTIONNAIRE 1•
YOUTH CULTURE

Directions

Answer the following questions yourself, according to what is true in your culture. Or use the following questionnaire to interview a classmate from another culture.

1. Do most parents in your culture feel that teenagers are difficult to control or to get along with?

2. If parents and teenagers disagree, what might they disagree about?

3. Do you or did you rebel as a teenager? In what ways? How did your parents react?

4. Would you say that teenagers in your culture have all the freedom that they want? Explain.

5. Do young people dress differently from older people? If so, how?

6. Do young people ever do the same dances as their parents? Do they have their own dances? Name some.

7. What is the most popular music among young people? Give examples.

8. Do you think young people today have different values from their parents? How so?

9. Do you think young people today have different politics from their parents? Explain.

10. Do young people have any special phrases or words that their parents wouldn't use?

11. What other differences have you noticed between younger and older people in your culture?

12. What aspects of American youth culture are popular among young people in your culture?

Name: _____ Culture: _____

• QUESTIONNAIRE 2•
AMERICAN YOUTH CULTURE

Directions

Interview an American between the ages of 15 and 25. Make up one question of your own at the end. Write down in the space at the end any new vocabulary that you learn in the interview.

1. Do most American parents feel that teenagers are difficult to control or to get along with?

2. If parents and teenagers disagree, what might they disagree about?

3. Do you or did you rebel as a teenager? In what ways? How did your parents react?

4. Would you say that American teenagers have all the freedom that they want? Explain.

5. Do American young people dress differently from older people? How?

6. Do American young people ever do the same dances as their parents? Do they have their own dances? Name some.

7. What is the most popular music among young people? Give examples.

8. Do you think young people today have different values from their parents? How so?

9. Do you think young people today have different politics from their parents? Explain.

10. Do young people today have any special phrases or words that older people wouldn't use?

11. What other differences have you noticed between younger and older people in the United States today?

12. (Your own question)

Person interviewed: _____ Sex: _____

Age: _____ Ethnic background: _____

Place of birth: _____

New vocabulary

INDIVIDUAL ANALYSIS

1. Compare the answers given by the American you interviewed with the way young people act in your culture. On which questions are the answers similar?

2. On which questions are they different?

3. Did any of the American's answers surprise you? If so, how?

4. Is American youth culture popular among young people in your culture? If so, why?

GROUP ANALYSIS

Based on students' interviews and individual analyses, discuss the following questions in class:

1. In what ways are American young people like young people from other parts of the world? Be specific about countries.

2. In what ways are American young people most different from young people in other countries?

3. What are some ways that young people outside the United States have developed their own forms of youth culture?

4. Do American young people think they have all the freedom they want? Do you think that American young people's freedom fits in with the values of American society? Explain.

5. What are some of the most popular styles of dress, dance, music, and speech among American young people today? Did American young people who were interviewed from different ethnic and racial groups give the same answers, or do young people from different groups seem to have their own styles?

6. Did the Americans interviewed say their values were different from their parents'? In what ways? Do you think that these differences will last, or do you think that as they get older the young people will become more like their parents?

7. What aspects of American youth culture have become popular in other countries? Why?

8. What are some of the answers that Americans gave to question 12?

Additional Activities

DICTIONARY

Put together a dictionary of words and phrases popular among American youth today. For example, in some parts of the country, "a *wicked* good time" is used to mean "a very good time." Look over the answers to question 10 of your classmates' interviews with Americans, and talk to some other Americans yourself. Then make a dictionary of the words and phrases you found. For each, include the standard English meaning, the new meaning, and a sentence using the word.

WRITING ASSIGNMENT

Research and write an essay on one particular style, such as "preppie" or "punk," that is a part of American youth culture today. Include information about its heroes or stars, how and when it started, among which social classes and ethnic groups it is most popular, the dress, music, dances, language associated with it, and the values it represents.

FASHION SHOW

Together with other members of your class, put on a fashion show displaying some of the most extreme clothing styles in American youth culture today. Play appropriate music as you show off the clothes.

ROLE PLAY

Role-play the scene in the Donovan family. Then role-play the same situation as it might happen in a family from another culture.

DEBATE

Debate the following question in class: *American teenagers have too much freedom — yes or no?* Use information from the Americans you interviewed as well as the class discussion about life in other countries to support your arguments.

DANCE

Learn an American dance, and demonstrate it in class.

In Conclusion

Do you think that an international youth culture is developing? Explain.

Chapter 12

Your Own Topic

RELIGION ?
SUPERSTITIONS ?
PROFESSIONS

HOBBIES
MUSIC ?
SPORTS

HUMOR
PETS ?
DEATH ?

FRIENDSHIP ?
CHILDREN'S GAMES
CHILD RAISING

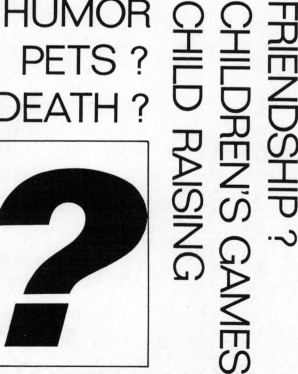

In this chapter, you will have the chance to do your own cross-cultural investigation. You will investigate, or find out about, any topic that you personally are very much interested in. You will use the same methods of interviews and analysis that you learned in other chapters of *Face to Face*. Then you will write your own case study, like the case studies in other chapters, to present to the class. Your case study will be about cultural differences that you learned about in the interviews.

Preparation

TOPIC

Choose any topic that you are interested in. On page 160 are some suggestions. But you do not have to pick from this list, if you have your own idea.

PREPARING YOUR QUESTIONNAIRES

You will make up a questionnaire of about 10 questions on your topic. Then you will make five copies of the questionnaire. One copy you will answer yourself, according to the customs of your own culture. You will then interview four Americans with the other questionnaires.

To make up a good questionnaire, follow these steps:

1. Think about some of the cultural similarities you think you might find. In what ways do you think people from your culture and Americans have similar customs and attitudes about your topic? Write some questions to find out if you are right about these similarities. For example, if you believe that Americans, like people from your culture, like to keep dogs as pets, write: "Do most Americans like to keep dogs as pets?"

2. Think about all the differences you think you might find between how Americans and people from your culture act and feel about your topic. Make up some questions to see if you are right about these differences.

3. Are there some things that Americans seem to do (related to your topic) that you do not understand completely? Make up questions to find out more about what confuses you.

4. Have you ever heard of any stereotypes of Americans that have to do with your topic? Make up questions to find out if the stereotypes have any truth to them.

5. Make up several questions about customs related to your topic. For example, ask who, what, where, when, how, or why people *do* certain things.

6. Make up several questions about attitudes related to your topic. For example, ask *how people feel* about certain things.

7. Now put together all your questions (you will probably have more than 10). Choose the 10 best. Be sure that some of the questions are about customs, and put these first. Other questions should be about attitudes or values, and these should be last.

8. Make sure that your questions are clear. Show them to an American or to your teacher and correct them if necessary.

9. Copy your questions neatly and make five copies of your questionnaire.

Interviews and Analysis

INTERVIEWS

First, fill out a questionnaire yourself, according to the customs and attitudes in your culture.

Then interview four Americans. If possible, choose Americans of different ages, sexes, and racial or religious groups.

ANALYSIS

Compare the answers on all five questionnaires:

1. What similarities did you find between Americans and your cultural group?

2. What differences did you find? Can you explain the reasons for any of these differences?

3. What differences did you find among the Americans you interviewed? Do you think that age, sex, race, or religion could explain any of these differences?

4. Did any of the answers help you understand American values better? Give an example of one or more American values that would help explain some American answers.

5. What answer or answers surprised you the most?

6. What kind of cultural conflict or misunderstanding might happen because of some of the differences you found out from your interviews?

7. Write down any new English vocabulary that you learned since the beginning of this chapter. Give the definition of each new word.

REPORT

Prepare an oral or written report, based on your answers to the questions above. Present a written report to your teacher and/or an oral report to a small group of classmates or to the class as a whole.

Case Study

PREPARATION

A case study is a little story like the ones at the beginning of each chapter in this book. Write your own case study from the information you found out in your interviews. The case study should be about a cultural conflict or misunderstanding between an American and someone from your cultural group. The cause of the misunderstanding should be some cultural difference related to your topic.

PRESENTATION

You can present your case study in written or in oral form:

Written Presentation

Write your case study in paragraph form. Remember, describe something that happens because of a cultural misunderstanding. Make up a happy ending. For example, write a solution for the conflict. Or have one of the people in the story explain the misunderstanding to the other so that they understand each other better.

Oral presentation (role play)

The idea for your role play should be something that happens because of a cultural misunderstanding (related to your topic). The role play should have a happy ending. That is, the people should come to understand each other and their misunderstanding by the end. Get some of your classmates to help you perform it. Then ask the rest of the class if they understood the reasons for the misunderstanding.

In Conclusion

Look over some of the questionnaires that you used in *Face to Face*. Consider the following questions:

1. What were some of the most surprising things that you learned since beginning the book?

2. Do you think your understanding of Americans has changed? Explain.

3. Do you think you understand better or feel differently about your own culture? Explain.

4. Look over the original list of questions your class put together at the beginning of the book. How many more can you answer now? Discuss your answers in class.